Austin Healey

1953-72

Austin Healey

100/4, 100/6, 3000 and Sprite MK. I-IV

1953-72

A Documentation by Walter Zeichner

Schiffer Publishing Ltd

1469 Morstein Road, West Chester, Pennsylvania 19380

This volume of the Schiffer Automotive Series is dedicated to the British Austin Healey 100/4, 100/6, 3000 and Sprite sports cars. This manufacturer's most important and interesting sales material has been chosen to portray an almost complete picture of an epoch that marked a high point in the era of British roadsters. Today they are all desirable collector cars, and many former owners of such cars will look through this book and say:

"If only I had never sold my Healey . . ." And those who own one will smile contentedly.

For their helpful support in assembling the documentation I would like to thank Messrs. Georg Amtmann, Rainer Simons and Robert Horender, as well as the Austin Rover Group, successor to the British Motor Corporation.

Halwart Schrader, Editor

Originally published under the title "Austin-Healey", 1953-72, Schrader Motor Chronik, copyright Schrader Automobil-Bücher, Handels-GmbH, München, West Germany, © 1986, ISBN: 3-922617-16-6.

Translated from the German by Dr. Edward Force.

Copyright © 1989 by Schiffer Publishing.
Library of Congress Catalog Number: 89-063366.

Printed in the United States of America.
ISBN: 0-88740-212-7

Published by Schiffer Publishing, Ltd.
1469 Morstein Road
West Chester, Pennsylvania 19380
Please write for a free catalog.
This book may be purchased from the publisher.
Please include $2.00 postage.
Try your bookstore first.

Contents

Using an Austin Healey to tow an oldtimer, a use as unusual as it is stylish...

Healey and Austin Healey—Classic British Sports Cars

The Englishman Donald Healey really did not have automobiles in mind when, at the age of sixteen, he volunteered for the Royal Flying Corps at the beginning of World War I to defend his country from the air. Only later, when his own country's anti-aircraft guns had shot him down, did his attitude toward flying change a bit, and Donald turned to earthbound vehicles. Shortly after the war he opened a garage in Perranporth, with financial help from his father, and soon began to get deeply interested in auto racing. With various vehicles that he modified for racing singlehandedly at his garage, he began to gain success and attract attention; in 1931, driving an Invicta, he even won the Monte Carlo Rally. In 1934 he began to work for Triumph as a test engineer, still driving in numerous races and rallies, winning almost half of them and rarely having to drop out early.

In 1946 Healey began his career as an independent car constructor, at first using part of a construction machine factory in Warwick as his construction site. The first Healey sports car had a 2.4-liter Riley motor as its powerplant, its body had been tested in a wind tunnel. The sport sedan version of the car ranked among the fastest British passenger cars of the early postwar era.

All Healey cars were really racing sports cars disguised for street use and gained a reputation to match. In 1951 a big roadster with a 3-liter Alvis motor was introduced, whose sleek body lines already showed distinct elements of the later Healey 100, a forerunner of the Austin Healey, the design of which goes back to the end of that same year.

Up to that point the sports cars of the Healey marque had, to be sure, won a series of noteworthy victories, but production was limited to a few dozen examples. Returning from the USA with the conviction that the market there was ready to accept high-performance sports cars, Healey set himself the goal of building a very fast sports car that was also suitable for everyday use, a car that could go 100 miles per hour, was inexpensive to build, and was easy and not demanding for its owner to maintain.

Healey soon came to the conclusion that this goal could be attained only by beginning with his own light construction and using as many of other constructors' production parts as possible. Within a short time, Donald Healey and his equally dedicated son Geoffrey built a simple frame of two box-section members extending the whole length of the car, from which cross-shaped transverse members branched to carry the chassis-and body-strengthening sheet metal components. Independent suspension with triangular transverse links and coil springs for the front wheels contrasted with leaf-spring suspension for the rear axle; beyond that, they limited themselves chiefly to parts available from the Austin Motor Company. As a result, the 2660-cc four-cylinder motor, with its pushrod-activated overhead camshaft, came from the proven Austin A 90, but was equipped with two SU H4 carburetors, which made possible a performance of 90 HP at approximately 4000 rpm of the crankshaft. Likewise the Austin four-speed transmission was used, which was merely rebuilt to replace its unsporting steering-wheel shifting with a central floor shift, and even the tires were mounted on A 90 disc wheels.

The car, which bore the name of Healey 100, was ready in time for the 1952 London Auto Show. Its name was naturally meant to be a reference to its top speed. To be sure, the somewhat shy but effective light blue car did not exactly have the best place on the Healey display, standing half hidden by a

in Warwick could not have come anywhere near meeting the demand anyway, they soon reached an agreement, even before the London Motor Show had ended. From now on, Healey bore only the responsibility for development and design, and no longer had to worry about production and sales.

Above: Walter Hirsch driving an Austin Healey in a 1963 race for historic vehicles. An authentic competition car! Right: A Mark III with widened fenders, modified by Franco Sbarro in Switzerland.

column and very near the Spanish Pegaso super-sports car, a potential magnet to draw the public. But soon enough, large crowds of people gathered around the roadster with its simple but beautiful lines and long engine hood. In a short time it became necessary to hold the people back from the besieged Healey stand with barricades . . .

This commotion very quickly drew the attention of Austin's chief, Leonard Lord, who had already been following Healey's work with keen interest, all the more so as Healey had bought so many Austin parts. Lord soon decided to make Healey an offer to take over production of the very promising sports car, and since the capacity of Healey's small business

As 1953 began, some twenty Healey 100 pre-series cars were built in Warwick, while the prototype was winning prizes at auto shows in Miami and New York, where it was honored as International Show Car of the World.

After several tests, in which it was shown that the car was easily capable of exceeding the 100-mph mark, the first production Austin Healey 100's left the Longbridge factory, bearing the winged Austin emblem over their striking radiator grilles. It did not take long before the Austin Healeys took part in great international auto races, as in the 24 Hours of Le Mans in 1953, where two Austin Healeys finished second and third in their class. The Jaguar XK 120

7

and Aston Martin DB2, which had formerly been so dominant, now had a new rival to take seriously. In the Liége-Charbonnières-Liége Rally in the same year, an Austin Healey was in the first five when damage to the rear axle destroyed its hopes for a victory. Several international speed records were also set by the car, often driven by Donald Healey himself, for example 229.4 mph over a mile with a flying start, set by a production BN 1, as the car was known in the factory code.

Even before 1955, when the Type BN 2 appeared with several important improvements, one could buy, as of the summer of 1954, a particularly powerful production version called the 100 S, the S standing for Sebring, the well-known racecourse. This special type, intended mainly for competition, attained an impressive 132 HP thanks to extensive tuning measures such as a more precise camshaft, an aluminum cylinder head and increased compression, all concealed beneath aluminum bodywork. External identifying marks of this racer, of which only 55 were made, were cooling vents on the motor hood, the absence of bumpers, and a small air intake at the front; disc brakes on all four wheels provided safe slowing of this bundle of energy.

In August of 1955 the improved version of the Austin Healey 100 (factory code BN 2) was introduced; as yet nothing about the motor had changed, but the brakes had been improved along with the front axle, and a hypoid rear axle had been included, as had a gearbox with overdrive. Just two months later there was another special model, this time called the 100 M (Le Mans), specially equipped for racing with a strengthened chassis and roll bar, and a power of 110 HP. 1159 of them were produced, often for successful racing drivers, some of them sponsored by the factory.

When a new model was presented in March of 1956, some 15,000 of these fine cars had already been sold, mainly in the USA. Under the hood there was now a six-cylinder motor, producing 100 HP from a displacement of 2.6 liters, which at that time was also used in similar form in the Morris Isis and Austin Westminster family sedans. The 100/6, alias BN 4, went into production in March of 1956, immediately inspiring a wave of excitement with its high-performance and high-quality motor. For the important American market, places for two children were created behind the seats, which became possible by slightly lengthening the wheelbase, and the oval radiator grille now had vertical bars.

The next step in the development of this classic English sports car was an increase in performance to 117 HP by slightly increasing the compression and using larger carburetors. There were also refined versions of this BN 6, which produced more than 150 HP and put up a bitter fight on rally and race courses, but the production version, with a sustained speed of over 170 kph, was also a sports car to be taken seriously.

The high point of increased performance had not yet been reached, for in July of 1959 a new version of the Austin Healey appeared, with its engine bored out to a displacement of 2912 cc to make better use of the limits of the three-liter sports car class. The 124-HP Austin Healey 3000 existed as a two-seater (BN 7) or a 2+2 (BT 7) until 1961, when its replacement appeared in the form of the 3000 Mark II, whose motor produced 132 HP with the help of a triple carburetor, making for more flexibility and better acceleration. From April 1962 to February 1964 this 3000 Mark II, called BJ 7 at the factory, was available only in 2+2 form, its double carburetor producing 12 more horsepower, and its use of a new gearbox

Left: An Italian sports car fan's Sprite Mark I. Below: A Sprite Mark II with hardtop, built in 1962, owned by a collector from Rosenheim, Germany.

offering the driver considerably more foot space. The cars also had cranked windows (only snap-on panels until then), and the spoked wheels available optionally for an extra charge were strengthened from 48 to 60 spokes. Finally, as of February 1964 the last and also most powerful version of the big Austin Healey was offered, the Mark III, with a larger double carburetor, more precise camshaft and overworked inlet ducts, giving a performance of 148 HP, enough to let the car in its production form just exceed the 200-kph mark. The decidedly businesslike atmosphere of earlier models no longer dominated the dashboard; instead, hardwood veneer even gave a touch of luxury, and the back seats could be folded down to create space for large luggage. Shortly after production began, the exhaust system was even improved, apparently the only part of the Austin Healey 3000 that had attracted complaints steadily since 1953.

The end came for this milestone among postwar

sports cars in 1967, in the form of increasingly stringent safety regulations in the USA, the Austin Healey's main customer. Satisfying these regulations would have resulted in such extensive and expensive changes that not much of the original construction

9

would have remained. After 14 years of fruitful cooperation, Healey separated from Austin to work on a new sports car project for Jensen.

But the big Austin Healey was not the only car that Donald Healey, now 89 years old, created for Austin. In 1958, in fact, a tough and extremely Spartan little roadster called the Sprite had appeared, rounding off the program of Austin sports cars at the lower end. The little 46-HP four-cylinder car with 948-cc displacement had, as its styling peculiarity, its headlights sitting on the front hood, which soon won it the nickname of "Frogeye", and it did without such universal features as door locks and handles and a glove-compartment lid. Once one had squeezed into the narrow cockpit, practically inaccessible to big people, one could enjoy all road and motor noises almost unmitigated, and one always had exact information about weather conditions thanks to the primitive top. Despite all that, the little speedster naturally had a lot of charm, and the low price, under 7000 Marks at the time, helped the lively little car find many fans.

In 1961 this version was replaced by the tamer Mark II, in which the headlights were located more conventionally and, in fact, rather boringly, but this had been requested by numerous interested parties (and authorization officials), and the luggage space inside the likewise redesigned rear end could now be loaded via a trunk lid.

One year later a more powerful version of the Sprite came on the market, with an 1100-cc motor producing 56 HP and capable of moving the two-seater at almost 150 kph. Whoever was not satisfied with this could increase his Sprite's speed with various tuning packages from BMC, of which Austin was now a part, or other firms. Versions with more than 80 HP were no rarity. Within the firm there had meanwhile appeared competition in the form of the almost identical MG Midget, and the two types from the same firm now fought for the customer's favor.

In 1964 a Mark III was introduced, producing 3 HP more power, and in 1956 the final version, Mark IV followed, with the 65-HP motor of the Mini Cooper S, good for 160 kph. Meanwhile the car had given up some of its Spartan exterior; the interior had been more richly furnished, while cranked windows and a sufficiently weathertight top let even less toughened types make friends with the Austin Healey Sprite, which was still available with slight external changes as the MG Midget.

The Sprite was still built until 1972 (the Midget, in fact, until 1979), and the Sprites and Midgets achieved considerable success in international auto racing with, among others, Stirling Moss and Bruce McLaren at the wheel.

With the large and small Austin Healey sports cars, a series of very typically English sports cars came to an end, with no successors left to carry on. They were often uncompromising sports cars, modified for the everyday owner, with inimitable charm. And everyone who has the good fortune to own and drive such a car today will only smile softly at concepts like turbochargers and on-board computers . . .

Winter-weathertight or not—Austin Healey 3000 Mark III with spoked wheels (Oldtimer Garage, Bern), built in 1967.

Below: A sports car developed by Healey in 1950-51 for Nash, the American automobile manufacturer; it also ran at Le Mans.

THE "MILLE MIGLIA" ROADSTER

No apology is needed for the use of the name "Mille Miglia" as a prefix to the Roadster and Saloon, as in this great Race both these models put up such outstanding performances

"the Fastest Car in the World IN SERIES PRODUCTION" — The Motor

Even in 1948, when this brochure was distributed, the "Mille Miglia" and "Sportsmobile" models were rarities in everyday traffic. Both models were powered by increased-performance Riley motors.

THE "SPORTSMOBILE" DROP-HEAD COUPE

SOME SPORTS EXPERTS' OPINIONS.

" An engineering triumph for Britain." *The Motor Magazine.*

" The Healey Saloon has the enviable distinction of having proved the fastest production car on any market in the world." *Motor Sport.*

" A sports car par excellence." *The Autocar.*

" Holds the road like a leech, a very fast car that can trickle through traffic smoothly and quietly. I have never driven a sports car I have liked better." *Sporting Life.* T. H. Wisdom.

" No car can have added as much to British prestige abroad in so short a time as the Healey by these brilliant performances." *The Motor.*

" The Healey employ the $2\frac{1}{2}$ litre Riley Engine — is the fastest standard unsupercharged car in the world." *Continental Daily Mail.*

" An 111-m.p.h. British Car beautifully designed." *Daily Mail.*

COMPLETE   ACH

After the splendid premiere of the Healey 100 at the 1952 London Auto Show, actual series production began in May of the following year. The Austin Healey 100/4, now built under Austin direction, soon won noteworthy success in racing and rallying and made sporting drivers' hearts beat faster during its long production run, in which it underwent numerous modifications. On the other hand, few people know that there were sporting sedans and roadsters bearing the Healey name in the Forties, built in very limited numbers, to be sure, but always highly regarded. And a Healey was also designed for the American firm of Nash in 1950!

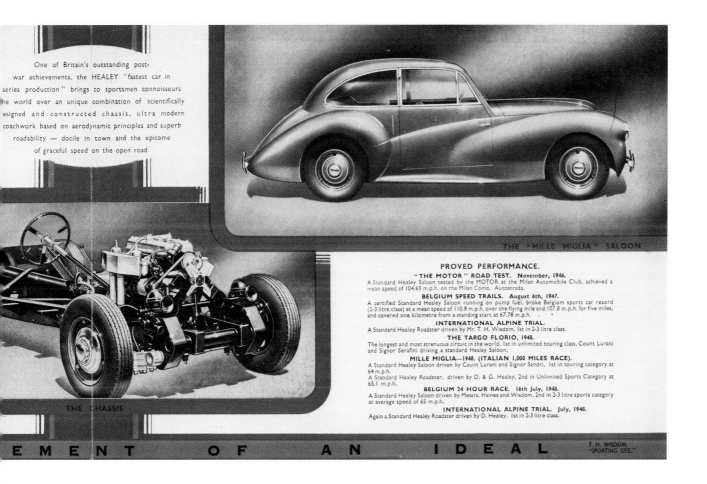

One of Britain's outstanding post-war achievements, the HEALEY "fastest car in series production" brings to sportsmen connoisseurs the world over an unique combination of scientifically designed and constructed chassis, ultra modern coachwork based on aerodynamic principles and superb roadability — docile in town and the epitome of graceful speed on the open road.

THE "MILLE MIGLIA" SALOON

THE CHASSIS

PROVED PERFORMANCE.

"THE MOTOR" ROAD TEST. November, 1946.
A Standard Healey Saloon tested by the MOTOR at the Milan Automobile Club, achieved a mean speed of 104.65 m.p.h. on the Milan Como. Autostrada.

BELGIUM SPEED TRAILS. August 6th, 1947.
A certified Standard Healey Saloon running on pump fuel, broke Belgium sports car record (2-3 litre class) at a mean speed of 110.8 m.p.h. over the flying mile and 107.8 m.p.h. for five miles, and covered one kilometre from a standing start at 67.78 m.p.h.

INTERNATIONAL ALPINE TRIAL.
A Standard Healey Roadster driven by Mr. T. H. Wisdom, 1st in 2-3 litre class.

THE TARGO FLORIO, 1948.
The longest and most strenuous circuit in the world, 1st in unlimited touring class, Count Lurani and Signor Serafini driving a standard Healey Saloon.

MILLE MIGLIA—1948. (ITALIAN 1,000 MILES RACE).
A Standard Healey Saloon driven by Count Lurani and Signor Sandri, 1st in touring category at 64 m.p.h.
A Standard Healey Roadster, driven by D. & G. Healey, 2nd in Unlimited Sports Category at 65.1 m.p.h.

BELGIUM 24 HOUR RACE. 16th July, 1948.
A Standard Healey Saloon driven by Messrs. Haines and Wisdom, 2nd in 2-3 litre sports category at average speed of 65 m.p.h.

INTERNATIONAL ALPINE TRIAL. July, 1948.
Again a Standard Healey Roadster driven by D. Healey. 1st in 2-3 litre class.

E M E N T   O F   A N   I D E A L

T. H. WISDOM.
"SPORTING LIFE."

Specification

2.4 LITRE

ENGINE. Manufactured by RILEY (Coventry) Ltd. Four-cylinder in line. Bore 80.5 mm. (3.16-inch) x Stroke 120 mm. (4.7-inch). 2,443 c.c. (140 c.u. inch). R.A.C. rating, 16.07 h.p. **Crankshaft** of special design, counterbalanced. $2\frac{1}{2}$-inch diameter bearings. **Cylinder Head**—Detachable. Hemispherical fully machined combustion chambers. "Straight-through" ports. **Valves**—O.H.V., 2 per cylinder at 90 degs. Of silicon-chrome steel. Push rod operated. **Connecting Rods** of special alloy steel. **Pistons**—Aluminium Alloy with large diameter gudgeon pins. **Camshafts**—Two high-level. Roller chain driven with automatic tensioner. **Lubrication**—Forced throughout. Positively driven high capacity pump, circulation through filter. Large size Light Alloy sump. **Ignition**—By coil and distributor with automatic and manual advance and retard. **Cooling**—Sealed pressure type. Circulation by pump and thermo-syphon with by-pass thermostat control. "Cross-flow" cooling in cylinder head **Carburation**—Two horizontal S.U. carburetters, specially tuned and with manual choke and throttle control. Special air silencer. **Exhaust system**—Special design for minimum back-pressure with Light Alloy tail pipe.

FRAME. Scientifically designed of immense strength, for light-weight. Box section throughout. Straight side-members, 6-inch deep "Cruciform" bracing.

SUSPENSION. Front—Independent of "Trailing Link" type incorporating vertical coil springs and large pressure-recuperating hydraulic dampers. **Rear**—Vertical coil springs and large pressure-recuperating hydraulic dampers mounted on light rigid banjo type rear axle.

TRANSMISSION. Clutch—Borg and Beck single plate 10-inch air-cooled. **Gearbox**—Four-speed and reverse. Synchro-mesh on second, third and top. Remote control central change speed lever. Accessible filling orifice with dip stick. Gear ratios—Top 3.5, 3rd 4.963, 2nd 7.542, 1st 12.761, Reverse 12.761. **Rear Axle**—Torque tube type with constant velocity needle roller bearing double universal joint. Axle located against side thrust by radius arm on rubber bushes.

BRAKES. 11-inch x $1\frac{3}{4}$-inch. Front, Lockheed Two-leading Shoe. 10-inch x $1\frac{3}{4}$-inch Rear. Hydraulic on all four wheels. Handbrake operates rear wheels only via cables. Large nickel chrome iron alloy ribbed drums.

STEERING. Exclusive steering layout (patented). Light yet positive at all speeds. "High-efficiency" type gear. Column adjustable. Large diameter thin rim spring steering wheel.

WHEELS AND TYRES. Dunlop Special light disc wheels, extra wide base. All wheels balanced. **Tyre equipment**—Dunlop Extra Low Pressure, size 5.75 x 15. and 6.00 x 15.

FUEL SYSTEM. 13-gallon rear mounted petrol tank with concealed filler. Twin electric pumps. Independent $1\frac{1}{2}$-gallon reserve supply with dash warning device.

ELECTRICAL EQUIPMENT. 12-volt with automatic voltage control and ventilated dynamo. 63 amp. battery. Special fully-recessed powerful headlamps. Foot-operated dipper switch. Two built-in Fog and Pass lights. Built-in twin tail lamps. Stop and Reversing Lights. Twin blended note wind-type horns. Twin-blade self-parking silent screen wipers. Concealed instrument lighting.

INSTRUMENTS. 5-inch 120 m.p.h. speedometer. 5-inch revolution counter, ammeter, oil pressure gauge, electrical petrol gauge, water temperature gauge, electric clock, petrol reserve warning light.

UPHOLSTERY AND CARPETING. All seats upholstered in best quality water-proofed Hide on Dunlopillo. Front seats fully adjustable.

SPARE WHEEL AND TOOLS. Spare wheel carried on rear locker with wheel-changing tools. Other tools accommodated in scuttle.

JACKING SYSTEM. Both wheels on either side may be raised clear of the ground with minimum effort from within the car in 15 seconds by the special "Bevelift" Jack.

BODY DETAILS. Aerodynamic shaped body with Aluminium Alloy panels. Wings, valances and bonnet also Light Alloy. **Bonnet**—Alligator type, incorporating special safety lock. Lock for bonnet operated from within the car.
Radiomobile is a standard fitting to the Sportsmobile. Provision is made for fitting Radiomobile to all other models at an inclusive cost of £40 0s. 0d.

PRINCIPAL DIMENSIONS.

	ft.	in.		ft.	in.
Wheel Base	8	6	Overall Length	14	1
Track—Front	4	6	Width	5	5
Rear	4	5	Height	4	10
Ground Clearance		7			

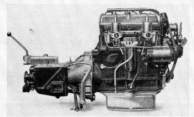

ENGINE

COLOUR RANGE. The colour schemes listed here are standard, and any deviations involving special treatment of exterior or upholstery will entail an extra charge. The cost being forwarded on application.

EXTERIOR :
Metallic Pearl Green.
„ Silver Blue.
„ Silver Grey.
„ Maroon.

INTERIOR :
Red, Maroon, Brown and Beige.
Blue.
Blue and Maroon.
Beige.

The Company reserves the right to alter or amend this Specification without previous notice.

FRONT SUSPENSION

DONALD HEALEY MOTOR COMPANY LIMITED, THE CAPE, WARWICK, ENGLAND.

Dans huit courses à longues distances des voitures HEALEY ont gagné 8 premiers prix, 4 seconds et 1 quatrième.

In acht Langstrecken-Prüfungen gewannen HEALEY Automobile 8 erste, 4 zweite und 1 vierten Preis.

1947	I. Pr.	RALLYE INT. DES ALPES (Cat. 2—3 lt)
1948	I. Pr.	RALLYE INT. DES ALPES (Cat. 2—3 lt)
	I. Pr.	TARGA FLORIO (Cat. Touring)
	I. Pr.	MILLE MIGLIA (Cat. Touring)
	II. Pr.	„ „ (Cat. Sport)
1949	I. Pr.	RALLYE INT. DES ALPES (Cat. 2—3 lt)
	II. Pr.	

TEAM PRICE «DAILY EXPRESS INT. TROPHY RACE»

(Voitures de série / Serienwagen)

1950	I. Pr.	FLORIDA RACE (Cat. 3 lt)
	II. Pr.	„ „ (Cat. 3 lt)
	II. Pr.	„ „ (Classification générale / Gesamtklassifikation)

En Octobre 1948 une Limousine HEALEY couvrait 166.950 km (103.76 mls) en une heure
(Contrôlé par Automobile Club de France)

Im Oktober 1948 fuhr eine HEALEY Limousine in einer Stunde 166.950 km (103.76 Meilen)
(Unter Kontrolle des Automobile Club de France)

ELLE DOMINE ◆ DER SIEGREICHE

In eight long-distance races, HEALEY cars won 8 first, 4 second and 1 fourth place.
(...1949 Daily Express...)
(Production cars)
(1950 Florida race...)
(Overall classification)
In October of 1948 a HEALEY sedan covered 166.950 km (103.76 miles) in one hour (under control of the Automobile Club of France)
THE VICTORIOUS
Motor: Manufactured by RILEY MOTORS LTD. 4 cyl. in line, 80.5 x 120 mm, 2443 cc, 2 SU "H4" horizontal carburetors.
Front suspension: Independent longitudinal links and coil springs, hydraulic shock absorbers.
Rear axle: Ratio 3.50:1 or optionally 3.25:1/3.0:1/4.1:1. Brakes: LOCKHEED hydraulic. Front 28 x 1.9 cm. Two primary shoes. Rear 25.4 x 1.9 cm. Hand brake operates mechanically on rear wheels.
Wheels and tires: Particularly light disc wheels with ventilating openings. Wide rims. Balanced wheels. Low-pressure tires: 5.50 x 15 / 5.75 x 15 / 6.00 x 15 / 6.50 x 15 / 6.40 x 15.
Fuel tank: Rear, approximately 70 liters.

Excerpt from an extremely rare brochure for the "Silverstone" type, introduced in 1949, which—powered by the same Riley motor--was intended mainly for racing. The wheels with their bicycle-type fenders and the partly folding windshield give the car an aggressive appearance.

Main dimensions: Wheelbase 2.59 meters (8'6")
Front track 1.37(4'6")
Rear track 1.35(4'5")
Overall length 4.26(14')
Overall width 1.60(5'3")
Overall height 1.09(3'7")
Available as chassis or sports two-seater. Colors: red/beige, green/beige.
The right to make modifications at any time is reserved.

HEALEY „SILVERSTONE" 2.4 Lt
DONALD HEALEY MOTOR CO. LTD. · THE CAPE · WARWICK · ENGLAND

Moteur : Produit par RILEY MOTORS LTD. 4 cyl. en ligne. 80,5 x 120 mm, 2443 ccm. Deux carburateurs SU horizontaux, «H4».

Suspension AV : Roues indépendantes. Manivelles longitudinales et ressorts à boudin. Amortisseurs hydrauliques.

Pont : Démultiplication du couple 3,50:1 ou sur demande 3,25:1 / 3,0:1 / 4,1:1.

Freins : Hydrauliques LOCKHEED. AV. 28 x 1,9 cm. Deux mâchoires primaires. AR. 25,4 x 1,9 cm. Frein à main mécanique sur roues AR.

Roues et Pneumatiques : Disques ultra-légers, ouvertures de refroidissement. Jantes larges. Roues équilibrées. Pneumatiques à faible pression: 5.50 x 15 / 5.75 x 15 / 6.00 x 15 / 6.50 x 15 / 6.40 x 15.

Bidon : 70 lt. à l'AR.

Motor : Hersteller RILEY MOTORS LTD. 4 Zyl. in Linie. 80,5 x 120 mm, 2443 ccm, 2 SU Vergaser horizontal, «H4».

Vorderradabfederung : Unabhängige Längsträger und Spiralfedern. Hydraulische Stossdämpfer.

Hinterachse : Übersetzung 3,50:1 oder auf Wunsch 3,25:1 / 3,0:1 / 4,1:1.

Bremsen : LOCKHEED hydraulisch. Vorn 28 x 1,9 cm. Zwei Primärbacken. Hinten 25,4 x 1,9 cm. Handbremse mechanisch auf Hinterräder.

Räder und Pneumatik : Besonders leichte, mit Ventilationsöffnungen versehene Scheibenräder. Breite Felgen. Räder ausgewuchtet. Niederdruck-Reifen: 5.50 x 15 / 5.75 x 15 / 6.00 x 15 / 6.50 x 15 / 6.40 x 15.

Benzintank : Hinten, ca. 70 lt.

Mesures principales / Hauptabmessungen:		
Empattement / Radstand :	2.59 mt	(8' 6")
Voie AV. / Spur vorne :	1.37	(4' 6")
AR. hinten :	1.35	(4' 5")
Longueur totale / Gesamtlänge :	4.26	(14')
Largeur totale / Gesamtbreite :	1.60	(5' 3")
Hauteur totale / Gesamthöhe :	1.09	(3' 7")

Livrable en châssis ou deux-places sport. Couleurs: rouge/beige vert/beige

Lieferbar als Chassis oder Sportzweisitzer. Farben: rot/beige grün/beige

Le droit de modifier les spécifications est réservé.   Änderungen jederzeit vorbehalten.

After another big sports car with a 3-liter Alvis motor was built in 1951, the developmental work of the Healey team concentrated completely on finishing the promising Type 100, which was sure to cause particular excitement on the American market, where European sports cars were highly desired.

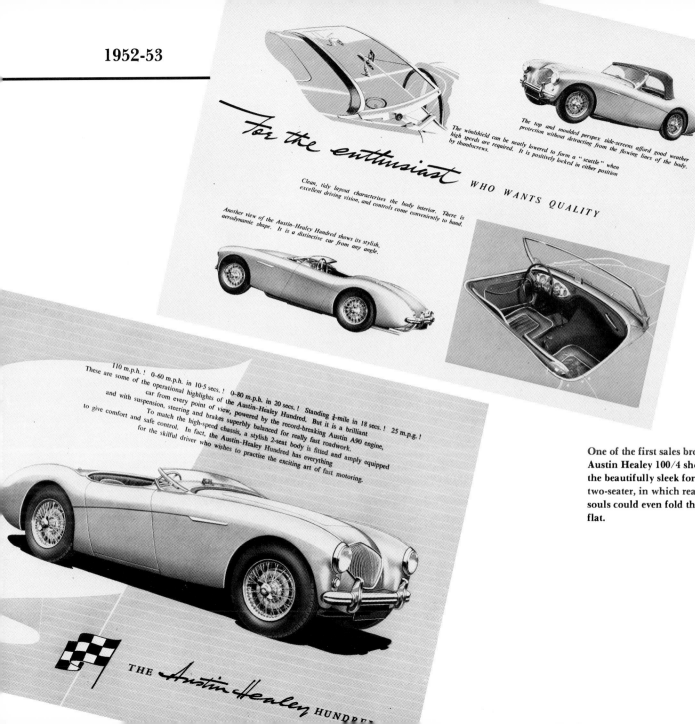

The windshield can be neatly lowered to form a "scuttle" when high speeds are required. It is positively locked in either position by thumbscrews.

The top and moulded perspex side-screens afford good weather protection without detracting from the flowing lines of the body.

For the enthusiast WHO WANTS QUALITY

Clean, tidy layout characterises the body interior. There is excellent driving vision, and controls come conveniently to hand.

Another view of the Austin–Healey Hundred shows its stylish, aerodynamic shape. It is a distinctive car from any angle.

110 m.p.h.! 0–60 m.p.h. in 10·5 secs.! 0–80 m.p.h. in 20 secs.! Standing ¼-mile in 18 secs.! 25 m.p.g.! These are some of the operational highlights of the Austin–Healey Hundred. But it is a brilliant car from every point of view, powered by the record-breaking Austin A90 engine, and with suspension, steering and brakes superbly balanced for really fast roadwork. To match the high-speed chassis, a stylish 2-seat body is fitted and amply equipped to give comfort and safe control. In fact, the Austin–Healey Hundred has everything for the skilful driver who wishes to practise the exciting art of fast motoring.

THE *Austin Healey* HUNDRED

One of the first sales brochures for the **Austin Healey 100/4** shows impressively the beautifully sleek form of the racy two-seater, in which really inspired souls could even fold the windshield flat.

17

SPECIFICATION

ENGINE : Bore 3·4375 in. (87·3 mm.) ; stroke 4·375 in. (111·1 mm.) ; capacity 162·2 cu. in. (2660 c.c.) ; b.h.p. 90 at 4,000 r.p.m.; maximum torque 144 lb./ft. at 2,000 r.p.m.; compression ratio 7·5 to 1.

Cylinders : Four cylinders cast integral with crankcase. Full length water jackets. Cast-iron cylinder head carrying all valve gear.

Crankshaft : Forged-steel, counterbalanced crankshaft supported in three detachable steel-backed white-metal bearings.

Connecting Rods : Forged steel with detachable steel-backed white-metal big-end bearings.

Pistons : Split-skirt type in low expansion aluminium alloy with alumilite finish. Three compression rings and one oil control ring fitted.

Camshaft : Forged steel, supported in three detachable steel-backed white-metal bearings. Cams of patented design for quiet operation. Driven by duplex roller chain from crankshaft with oil catchers and a tensioner ring of synthetic rubber to maintain chain lubrication and tightness respectively.

Valves : Overhead valves operated by push-rods. Large inlet valves of silicon chrome steel ; exhaust valves in " XB " steel designed to resist corrosion from leaded fuels.

Lubrication : Pressure gear pump forces oil to all main, big-end, camshaft and overhead-valve rocker-shaft bearings. Holes in the big-end bearings provide for jet lubrication of the cylinder walls, and the front camshaft bearing provides a controlled feed of oil to the timing chain. Both main and big-end bearing oil feeds are of patented design which ensures longer crankshaft life. A full-flow filter with renewable element is fitted. Oil capacity approximately 11¾ pints (6·68 litres).

Cooling : Circulation by centrifugal type of pump with thermostat control. Fan-cooled patented radiator to prevent loss of coolant through expansion. Water is directed to sparking plug bosses and exhaust port walls. Cooling system capacity 19 pints (10·8 litres).

Fuel System : Fuel from a rear tank of 10½ gallons (47·7 litres) capacity is fed by an S.U. electrical pump to twin S.U. carburetters fitted with air cleaners.

Ignition : Coil and battery ignition with automatic advance and retard and additional vacuum control.

Dynamo : 12-volt fan-ventilated unit with compensated voltage control.

Starter : Operated by push-button solenoid type of switch.

CLUTCH : Flexible dry single-plate Borg and Beck clutch is fitted, with spring cushion drive. Clutch diameter 9 in. (0·23 m.).

GEARBOX : Three forward speeds and reverse controlled by a short central gear lever and with synchromesh engagement for all gears. Oil capacity 5¼ pints (3·13 litres).

OVERDRIVE : An overdrive unit is fitted behind the gearbox and engaged by a control switch mounted on the fascia panel. The overdrive may be engaged in any gear, which in effect provides a choice of six gear ratios. An over-ride governor prevents accidental use of the overdrive at low speed.

PROPELLER SHAFT : Hardy Spicer propeller shaft with needle roller bearing universal joints. Lubrication nipples to each joint and to the sliding splines.

REAR AXLE : Spiral bevel three-quarter floating in a banjo-type casing. The pinion is carried by pre-loaded taper roller bearings. Oil capacity 2½ pints (1·42 litres).

OVERALL GEAR RATIOS : Without overdrive—9·28, 5·85 and 4·125, with 20·53 reverse. **With overdrive engaged**—7·61, 4·79 and 3·38.

ROAD SPEEDS AT 1,000 R.P.M.: Without overdrive—Top 18 m.p.h ; second 12·8 m.p.h.; first 8 m.p.h. **With overdrive engaged**—Top 23·8 m.p.h.; second 17 m.p.h.; first 10·6 m.p.h.

STEERING : Burman cam and lever steering gear. Diameter of steering wheel 16½ in. (0·42 m.). The steering wheel is adjustable for reach.

SUSPENSION : Front—Independent coil springs controlled by double-acting hydraulic shock absorbers interconnected by an anti-roll torsion bar. **Rear**—Semi-elliptic springs controlled by double-acting hydraulic shock absorbers and track bar.

BRAKES : Girling hydraulic with two leading shoes in front. Brake-drum diameter 11 in. (0·28 m.). Total frictional area 145·2 sq. in. (935 sq. cm.).

WHEELS AND TYRES : Wire-spoke knock-on wheels with 5·90—15 tyres.

ELECTRICAL : Two 6-volt batteries of 63 ampere-hour capacity at 10-hour rate ; positive earth ; built-in head-, side- and twin tail-lamps ; twin windshield wipers ; directional flashing lights available to conform with U.S. regulations ; twin horns.

INSTRUMENTS : Oil and fuel gauges ; water temperature gauge ; 120 m.p.h. speedo-meter ; 0–6,000 r.p.m. tachometer.

COACHWORK : Open two-seater with full-width individual bucket seats ; large enclosed rear luggage compartment ; full weather protection, including folding wind-shield, disappearing hood and detachable moulded perspex side-screens.

OVERALL DIMENSIONS : Wheelbase 7 ft. 6 in. (2·29 m.) ; track at front 4 ft. 0¾ in. (1·24 m.) ; track at rear 4 ft. 1½ in. (1·26 m.) ; overall length 12 ft. 2 in. (3·71 m.) ; overall width 5 ft. (1·52 m.) ; height over scuttle 2 ft. 11 in. (0·89 m.) ; height over windshield 3 ft. 11 in. (1·19 m.) ; height over hood 4 ft. 1 in. (1·24 m.) ; ground clearance 7 in. (0·18 m.) ; turning circle 30 ft. (9·14 m.) ; approximate dry weight 1,900 lb. (862 kg.).

THE AUSTIN MOTOR COMPANY LIMITED
LONGBRIDGE . . . . BIRMINGHAM

AUSTIN MOTOR EXPORT CORPORATION LIMITED
LONGBRIDGE, BIRMINGHAM, and OXFORD STREET, LONDON, ENGLAND

In Association with the **DONALD HEALEY MOTOR COMPANY LIMITED, THE CAPE, WARWICK**

Printed in England

Publication No. 981

Left: under the hood, the 2.7-liter motor of the Austin A 90 did its work and powered the light roadster, even in this four-cylinder version, to noteworthy attainments.

THE *Austin Healey* 100

Two pages from a splendid sales catalog of the mid-Fifties awaken the desire to own such a car . .

The instrument panel of the
earlier large Austin-Healeys,
was very clean and
functional.

Der Austin-Healey '100', ein schnittiger und schneller Wagen in eleganter Karosserieform. Wo immer er sich zeigt, bildet er den Mittelpunkt des Interesses.

The Austin-Healey '100', a racy and speedy car with elegant body style. Wherever it is seen, it becomes the center of interest.

The splendidly appointed cockpit with its two comfortable seats for driver and passenger. All instruments are easy to see. Easy-to-use stick shift. The good view of the road, thanks to the low motor hood that curves downward at the front, is noteworthy.

Das vornehm gehaltene Cokpit mit seinen 2 bequemen Sitzen für Fahrer und Mitfahrer. Alle Instrumente gut übersichtlich angeordnet. Leicht bedienbare Stockschaltung. Auffallend ist die gute Uebersicht der Fahrbahn dank der niederen, nach vorn heruntergezogenen Motorhaube.

Die Windschutzscheibe kann halb schräg nach vorn abgeklappt werden. Rückfahrspiegel und Scheibenwischer bleiben in Normalposition.

The folding windshield was meant to add a little bit to the top speed; the two-piece snap-on windows for rainy days were very sporting.

Leicht montier- und demontierbare gebogene Seitenteile für beide Türen.

The windshield can be folded down halfway flat to the front. The rear-view mirror and windshield wipers stay in position.

Arched side pieces, easy to install and remove, for both doors.

In March of 1956 the Type 100 Six, with the six-cylinder motor of the Austin Westminster, went into production.

The Austin Healey " 100 Six " is good to look at in its dual-tone paint finish, the smooth, clean bodylines presenting a delightfully pleasing picture from all points of view.
To suit individual needs, there are numerous items of equipment such as heater, overdrive, and wire wheels which can be fitted at extra cost.   But whatever the choice, the new " 100-Six " cannot fail to be the centre of attraction and the subject of much favourable comment.

Aluminium framed side screens have one fixed and one sliding perspex panel for ventilation or hand signalling.

Easy to recognize by its new, cross-ribbed radiator grille, this successor model had a narrow seat in the back, which could hold two children or a third adult.

The powerful and quiet-running six-cylinder motor brought the performance up to 100 HP.

SPECIFICATIONS

Literleistung: 38,6 HP/ltr.

ENGINE: 2,639 c.c. (161.1 cu. in.): bore 3.125 in. (79.4 mm.): stroke 3.5 in. (89 mm.): b.h.p. 102 at 4,600 r.p.m.: maximum torque 142 lb. ft. at 2,400 r.p.m.: compression ratio 8.25 to 1.

Cylinders: Six cylinders cast integral with crankcase. Detachable cast-iron head carrying valve gear.

Crankshaft: Forged steel supported by four steel-backed white metal bearings.

Connecting Rods: Forged steel with steel-backed white metal bearings.

Pistons: Split-skirt, flat top pistons in aluminium alloy with tin-plated finish. Three compression rings and one slotted oil control ring fitted.

Camshaft: Forged steel in four steel-backed white metal bearings. Cams of patented design to give efficient and quiet operation. The camshaft gear is driven by duplex roller chain which has an integral oil feed and an automatic slipper type tensioner to maintain chain lubrication and tightness respectively.

Valves: Overhead, operated by push-rods and designed for silent operation. Valve oil seals are fitted.

Lubrication: Oil is forced under pressure to all main, connecting rod and camshaft bearings and to each tappet. It is also fed to the timing chain and overhead valve rocker gear. The connecting rods have jet holes to provide oil for cylinder walls when starting-up. Both main and connecting rod oil feeds are of patented design to ensure longer crankshaft life. A full-flow oil filter is fitted. It has a renewable element. Oil capacity approximately 12 pints (6.8 litres).

Cooling: Circulation by fan and centrifugal pump with thermostat control. Water is delivered to the cylinder block and thence to ample passages surrounding the valve pockets and sparking plugs. A 4-bladed fan is fitted to export models. Cooling system capacity approximately 20 pints (10.8 litres).

Ignition: Coil and 12-volt battery. Automatic advance and retard and built-in vacuum control.

Fuel System: Fuel from a rear tank is fed by electric pump to two S.U. carburetters fitted with "pancake" air cleaners. A stop-tap is provided on the fuel tank. Tank capacity 12 gallons (54.6 litres).

CHASSIS: Transmission:

Clutch: Single dry plate, 9 in. (0.23 m.) diameter.

Gearbox: Ratios: Reverse 4.176; First 3.076; Second 1.913; Third 1.333; Top 1.0. Oil Capacity: approximately 4 pints (2.27 litres). Change speed: short central lever on floor.

Propeller Shaft: Open, with needle roller bearing universal joints.

Rear Axle: Ratio: 3.91 to 1 (11/43). Oil Capacity: approximately 3 pints (1.7 litres).

Road Speeds at 1,000 r.p.m.: First 6.152 m.p.h.; Second 9.879 m.p.h.; Third 14.177 m.p.h.; Top 18.898 m.p.h.

Transmission with Overdrive: (Road Speed Tyres must also be fitted.)

Clutch: Single dry plate, 9 in. (0.23 m.) diameter.

Gearbox: Ratios: Reverse 4.176; First 3.076; Second 1.913; Third 1.333; Top 1.0; Overdrive Third 1.037; Overdrive Top 0.778. Change speed: short central lever on floor. Oil capacity: approximately 5¼ pints (2.98 litres), including overdrive.

Propeller Shaft: Open, with needle roller bearing universal joints.

Rear Axle: Ratio, with overdrive: 4.1 to 1 (10/41). Oil capacity: approximately 3 pints (1.7 litres).

Road Speeds at 1,000 r.p.m.: First 5.86 m.p.h.; Second 9.42 m.p.h.; Third 13.52 m.p.h.; Top 18.02 m.p.h.; Overdrive Third 17.39 m.p.h.; Overdrive Top 23.18 m.p.h.

Steering: Cam and Peg. Ratio: 14 to 1. Steering Wheel: 3 spring spokes, 16½ in. (0.42 m.) diameter.

Suspension: Front—Independent wishbones, coil springs, shock absorbers and stabilizing bar. Rear—Leaf springs, shock absorbers and panhard rod. Shock absorbers: Lever type, hydraulic.

Brakes: Girling hydraulic. 2 Leading-Shoe on front. Diameter: 11 in. × 2¼ in. wide.

Road Wheels: 15 in. × 4J, Ventilated Steel Disc. Fixing: 5 nuts. Tyres: 5.90—15, tubeless. Models having disc wheels and overdrive, and those having wire wheels, with or without overdrive will be fitted with Road Speed tyres.

Electrical: 12 volt, 51 ampere-hour capacity battery. For cold countries, America and Canada, 70 ampere-hour capacity battery. Headlamps with dipping switch and equipment to suit regulations of different countries. Combined side lamps and flashing direction indicators. Combined twin stop-tail lamps and flashing direction indicators. Concealed instrument panel lamps. Twin horns. Twin windscreen wipers.

Instruments: Trip speedometer. Revolution counter. Fuel gauge. Combined oil and water temperature gauge. Red warning lights indicate no dynamo charge and headlamp high beam position. Green warning light, indicating direction indicators working. Switches for starter, lighting, screen wiper, and control for windscreen washer (also for heater and overdrive when fitted) on instrument panel. Panel light switch on lower edge of fascia.

Coachwork: Occasional four-seater, two-door, open sports tourer with all-weather protection. Steel/aluminium construction. Bonnet top—with chrome grille vent to assist engine cooling—hinged at rear edge and supported in open position by a pivoted rod. Bonnet lock operated from inside car. Wide rear-opening doors fitted with outside handles, a private lock being incorporated in handle of driver's door. A large open pocket is provided in each door. Fixed curved windscreen of laminated plate glass fitted with double screen wipers. Folding hood of P.V.C. plastic material includes large transparent backlight and can be stored—with hood sticks—behind rear seats when not in use. A tonneau cover completely covers all seats but can be opened for driver only. Luggage compartment with lockable lid at rear, lined with Armacord and containing battery with master switch and spare wheel. Front and rear chrome bumpers. Twin rear reflectors. Adjustable front bucket seats, the backs of which tilt forward to give access to the rear seats. All instruments grouped on driver's side of fascia, grab handle on passenger side. Interior driving mirror and trimmed crash pad fitted to top of scuttle, behind windscreen. Parcel tray fitted below fascia. Flush fitting ash tray in centre transmission tunnel. Fascia finished in leathercloth. Fitted carpet over floor. Overriders fitted to bumpers. Seats trimmed with hide facings. Padded hide and leathercloth armrest between front bucket seats. Detachable side windows have polished alloy frames with one fixed and one sliding perspex panel. Windscreen washer. Paint finish in dual colours.

Optional extras: Radio. Hardtop. Heater. Electrically operated overdrive and Road Speed tyres. 15 in. × 4J wire spoke 'knock-on' wheels.

Leading Dimensions: Wheelbase 7 ft. 8 in. (2.336 m.); overall length 13 ft. 1½ in. (4.000 m.); overall height (hood up) 4 ft. 1 in. (1.244 m.); overall height (hood down) 3 ft. 10 in. (1.168 m.); overall width 5 ft. 0½ in. (1.536 m.); height over scuttle 2 ft. 11½ in. (0.914 m.); ground clearance 5½ in. (0.140 m.); track, front at ground level 4 ft. 0½ in. (1.238 m.); track, rear 4 ft. 2 in. (1.270 m.); turning circle 35 ft. 0 in. (10.668 m.); approximate unladen weight, with spare wheel and tyre, tools, oil and water, less fuel. (With 'knock-on' wire wheels and overdrive) 22 cwt. (1122 kg.).

Leistungsgewicht: 11 kg/HP

THE AUSTIN MOTOR COMPANY LIMITED
LONGBRIDGE . . . BIRMINGHAM

AUSTIN MOTOR EXPORT CORPORATION LIMITED
LONGBRIDGE . . BIRMINGHAM . . ENGLAND

Printed in England by Wills & Hepworth Ltd., Loughborough

Publication No. 1334

S

The sleek, smart, aerodynamic lines of the new " 100 Six " model delight the eye and the body provides seating for four, plus generous luggage space.

And power is there also—six cylinder power. For the Austin 2639 c.c. O.H.V. engine fitted with twin S.U. carburetters develops 102 b.h.p. and provides brilliant acceleration and sustained high cruising speed.

The remarkably ingenious design of the new four-seater Austin Healey " 100 Six " puts a 100 m.p.h.-plus performance at your disposal and you will marvel at the way the car holds the road, hugs the corners and eats up distance with effortless ease.

A classic example of British engineering at its best, this car will blaze a high speed trail of popularity along the highways of the world.

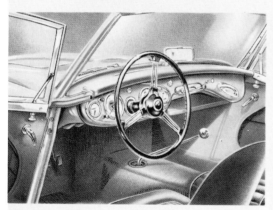

Still a sports car in the term's fullest meaning, the thrill of this type of motoring is now possible not only for you but for three other members of the family.

For ease of entry, forward hinged doors open wide and the lower edges lift well clear of the kerb or sidewalk. The wide, curved windscreen provides excellent vision ahead.

The dashboard in classic-English style and the folding top made the 100 Six into a car for people who could get along without great comfort. The other seats could be covered over to make a sort of single-seater, which was regarded as terribly sporty at that time.

Model

The new standard " 100 Six " is soundly designed from bumper to bumper. Power is transmitted through a four-speed synchromesh gearbox to the hypoid rear axle which carries ventilated pressed steel disc wheels fitted with 5.90—15 tubeless tyres.

A tough P.V.C.-fabric hood is included in the comprehensive all-weather equipment of the " 100 Six." Folded away behind the rear seat, it is speedily erected when necessary.

A snap-on tonneau cover is also provided, which can be opened for driver only or for driver and passenger—the rear seats remaining covered.

27

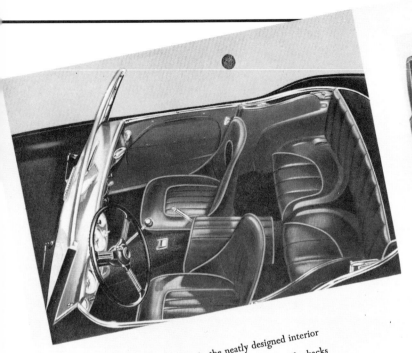

All instruments are easily readable, being closely grouped in a panel in front of the driver. On the opposite side of the covered fascia is a grab-handle for the convenience of the passenger.

The spare wheel and battery with master switch are stowed in the rear compartment and there is a surprising amount of space available for family luggage.

Each of the adjustable bucket seats in the neatly designed interior is upholstered in latex foam rubber, with hide facings. The backs tilt forward to give access to the rear seats.

Gears are selected by a short central gear lever and for driving comfort the 17-inch diameter wheel has spring spokes.

As well as a parcel shelf beneath the fascia, each door has an open pocket for personal items, and a hard wearing carpet over the entire floor completes the stylish interior trim.

'100 Six' De Luxe Model

The comfortable bucket seats offered a firm hold on fast curves, and one still sat comparatively close to the big three-spoked steering wheel . . .

The motor, with exactly 2639 cubic centimeters of displacement, was a model of elasticity and robustness, and caused the Austin Healey driver few problems as a rule.

A vibration damper is fitted externally on the forward end of the crankshaft.

Split skirt aluminium alloy pistons have three compression rings and one slotted oil control ring.

The timing chain is automatically adjusted by a slipper-type chain tensioner.

The robust, four-bearing, fully-balanced crankshaft.

The car still had production drum brakes.

Right: Hardtop and heater were also extras.

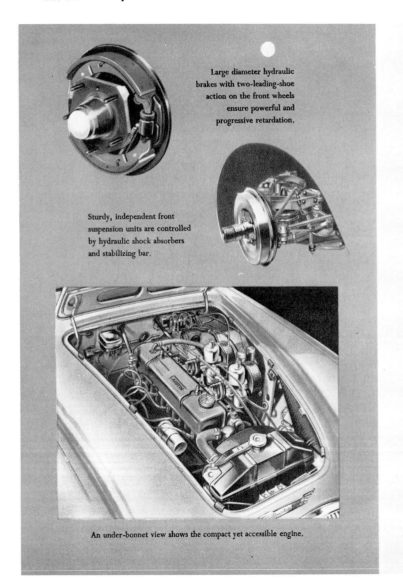

Large diameter hydraulic brakes with two-leading-shoe action on the front wheels ensure powerful and progressive retardation.

Sturdy, independent front suspension units are controlled by hydraulic shock absorbers and stabilizing bar.

An under-bonnet view shows the compact yet accessible engine.

A removable hard-top instantly gives to the "100 Six" the appearance and convenience of a sports saloon.

For extremely cold climates, a fresh air heater with demisters can be neatly installed.

OPTIONAL EXTRAS

A fully comprehensive range of optional extras and alternative equipment is available for the Austin Healey " 100 Six." Heater and demisters, radio, overdrive, hardtop, wire-spoke knock-on wheels and " Road Speed " tyres can all be fitted to order, at extra cost.

If you like a radio in your car, there is a set available which gives good reception in all countries of the world.

The NEW occasional four-seat sports tourer

The sparkling performance of the Austin Healey '100' in both private and competition trim brought it world-wide acclaim. And now, as a six-cylinder, four-seater sports tourer it must gain increased popularity.

Sleeker and smarter than ever, the clean, aerodynamic lines of the new '100 Six' are unaffected by the inclusion of two occasional rear seats—and there is still considerable space available in the luggage compartment.

In its standard form, the Austin Healey '100 Six' is equipped with ventilated pressed-steel disc wheels, but wire-spoked "knock-on"

wheels are available at extra cost. The four-speed synchromesh gear-box can, if desired, be fitted with an electrically operated overdrive, which not only provides high cruising speed, but effects considerable economy in fuel. A comprehensive range of optional extras can be fitted to suit the individual requirements of the enthusiast.

Here indeed is a first-class example of British engineering design and constructional skill at its best—a car to maintain the reputation for dependability and quality held by its forerunner.

In such a stylich atmosphere, and equipped with the spoked wheels available at extra charge, the sporting elegance of this classic English roadster comes across especially impressively. But the space for luggage in the trunk was severely limited by the spare wheel and the battery.

Since the big roadster not only attracted attention in the hands of sports-car inspired drivers on the open road, but also played an important role in international racing and rallying, the displacement was enlarged in 1959 to 2912 cc, in order to make the greatest possible use of the limits of the 3-liter sports car class. This two-seater or 2+2, called the Austin Healey 3000, was produced from July 1959 to the autumn of 1967, and its initial performance of 124 HP was increased to 148 HP in the last type built, the Mark III.

two-seater or occasional four-seater sports cars

Austin Healey 3000

Title page of the first Austin Healey 3000 brochure of 1959, with two-or four-seat versions.

The incomparable AUSTIN-HEALEY "3000"

New power-plus performance . . . . sleek aerodynamic lines . . . . a two-fold triumph for Austin-Healey. The powerful new B.M.C. 2.9 litre engine provides vivid acceleration and sustained high speeds in excess of 100 m.p.h. with synchromesh or overdrive gearbox, while disc brakes on the front wheels ensure safe, rapid deceleration and inspire confidence at all times. Fully equipped for all-weather motoring, it is unique in its class and price range. Here is a sports car for the motorways of the world, to carry you any distance, at speed with safety, in superb style and comfort. Single or dual tone paint finishes are available and there is a comprehensive range of optional equipment for the specialist-enthusiast.

Left- or right-hand drive . . . .

. . . . two- or occasional four-seater, and plenty of room for luggage in either version!

The pictures in this sales brochure also make clear that it was hard to find an angle from which the Austin Healey 3000 did not look good. The classic spoked wheels with central hubs were especially becoming.

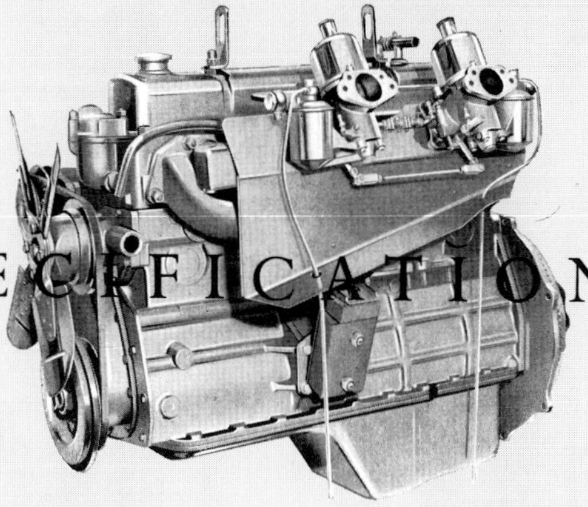

S P E C I F I C A T I O N

ENGINE: 2,912 c.c. (177.7 cu. in.); bore 3.282 in. (83.36 mm.); stroke 3.5 in. (89 mm.); b.h.p. 124 at 4,600 r.p.m. (nett); 130 b.h.p. at 4,750 r.p.m. (gross); maximum torque 175 lb. ft. at 3,000 r.p.m.; compression ratio 9.03 to 1.
Cylinders: Six cylinders cast integral with crankcase.
Cylinder Head: Detachable in cast-iron with separate six-port cast aluminium inlet manifold. Two-piece cast-iron exhaust manifold fitted with twin exhaust system.
Crankshaft: Forged steel support by four steel-backed white metal bearings.
Connecting Rods: Forged steel with steel-backed white metal bearings.
Pistons: Solid-skirt, flat top pistons in aluminium alloy with tin-plated finish. Three compression rings and one slotted oil control ring fitted.
Camshaft: Forged steel in four steel-backed white metal bearings. Cams of patented design to give efficient and quiet operation. The camshaft gear is driven by duplex roller chain, which has an integral oil feed and an automatic slipper type tensioner to maintain chain lubrication and tightness respectively.
Valves: Overhead, operated by push-rods and designed for silent operation. Valve oil seals are fitted. KE965 steel exhaust valves.
Lubrication: Oil is forced under pressure to all main, connecting rod and camshaft bearings and to each tappet. It is also fed to the timing chain and overhead valve rocker gear. The connecting rods have jet holes to provide oil for cylinder walls when starting up. Both main and connecting rod oil feeds are of patented design to ensure longer crankshaft life. A full-flow oil filter is fitted, which has a renewable element. Oil capacity approximately 12 pints (6.8 litres).
Cooling: Circulation by fan and centrifugal pump with thermostat control. Water is delivered to the cylinder block and thence to ample passages surrounding the valve pockets and sparking plugs. A 4-bladed fan is fitted to export models. Cooling system capacity approximately 20 pints (11.37) litres.
Ignition: Coil and 12 volt battery. Automatic advance and retard and built-in vacuum control.
Fuel System: Fuel from a rear tank is fed by electric pump to two semi-downdraught S.U. HD6 carburetters fitted with "pancake" air cleaners. A stop tap is provided on the fuel tank. Tank capacity 12 gallons (54.6 litres).

CHASSIS: Transmission:

Clutch: Single dry plate, 10 in. (0.25 m.) diameter.

Gearbox: Ratios: Reverse 3.78; First 2.93; Second 2.053; Third 1.309; Top 1.0 to 1. Oil capacity: approximately 4 pints (2.27 litres). Change speed: short central lever on floor.

Propeller Shaft: Open, with needle roller bearing universal joints.

Rear Axle: Ratio: 3.545 to 1 (11/39). Oil Capacity: approximately 3 pints (1.7 litres).

Road Speeds at 1,000 r.p.m.: First 7.15 m.p.h.; Second 10.2 m.p.h.; Third 16.0 m.p.h.; Top 20.9 m.p.h.

Transmission with Overdrive:

Clutch: Single dry plate, 10 in. (0.25 m.) diameter.

Gearbox: Ratios—Reverse 3.78; First 2.93; Second 2.053; Third 1.309; Overdrive Third 1.076; Top 1.0 to 1; Overdrive Top 0.822. Change speed: short central lever on floor. Oil capacity: approximately 5¼ pints (2.98 litres), including overdrive.

Propeller Shaft: Open, with needle roller bearing universal joints.

Rear Axle: Ratio, with overdrive: 3.91 to 1 (11/43). Oil capacity: approximately 3 pints (1.7 litres).

Road Speeds at 1,000 r.p.m.: First 6.475 m.p.h.; Second 9.24 m.p.h.; Third 14.47 m.p.h.; Overdrive Third 17.65 m.p.h.; Top 18.94 m.p.h.; Overdrive Top 23.1 m.p.h.

Steering: Cam and Peg. Ratio: 14 to 1. Steering Wheel: three spring spokes, 17 in. (0.43 m.) diameter.

Suspension: Front—Independent wishbones, coil springs, shock absorbers and stabilizing bar. Rear—Semi-elliptic leaf springs, shock absorbers and panhard rod. Hydraulic lever type shock absorbers.

Brakes: Girling hydraulic. 11¼ in. (0.29 m.) discs on front. Drum type 11 in. diameter × 2¼ in. wide on rear.

Road Wheels: 15 in. × 4J, Ventilated Steel Disc. Fixing: 5 nuts. Tyres: 5.90—15 Road Speed.

Electrical: 12 volt (consisting of two 6 volt batteries on 2-seater), 50 ampere hour capacity at 10 hour rate, (57 ampere hour at 20 hour rate). Headlamps with dipping switch and equipment to suit regulations of different countries. Combined side lamps and flashing direction indicators. Combined twin stop-tail lamps and flashing direction indicators. Concealed instrument panel lamps. Twin horns. Twin windscreen wipers.

Instruments: Trip speedometer. Revolution counter. Fuel gauge. Combined water temperature and oil pressure gauge. Red warning lights indicate no dynamo charge and headlamp high beam position. Green warning light shows direction indicators working. Switches for starter, lighting, screen wiper, and control for windscreen washer (also for heater and overdrive when fitted) on instrument panel. Panel light switch on lower edge of fascia. Windscreen washer.

Coachwork: Two- or four-seater, two-door, open sports tourer with all-weather protection. Steel/aluminium construction. Bonnet top—with chrome grille vent to assist engine cooling—hinged at rear edge and supported in open position by a pivoted rod. Bonnet lock operated from inside car. Wide rear-opening doors fitted with outside handles. A large open pocket is provided in each door. Fixed curved windscreen of laminated plate glass fitted with double screen wipers. Folding hood of vinyl treated fabric includes large transparent backlight which—with hood sticks—can be completely removed. A tonneau cover completely covers seats but can be opened for driver only. Luggage compartment with lockable lid at rear, lined with Armacord and containing spare wheel in special container over rear axle on two-seater, on floor of boot in four-seater. Front and rear chrome bumpers with overriders. Twin rear reflectors. Adjustable front bucket seats, the squabs of which tilt forward to give access to the rear compartment. Batteries in special locker beneath spare wheel container on two-seater and in luggage boot on four-seater. Master switch independently operated from inside luggage compartment. All instruments grouped on the driver's side of fascia, grab handle on passenger's side. Interior driving mirror and trimmed crash pad fitted to top of scuttle, behind windscreen. Parcel tray fitted below fascia. Flush fitting ash tray in centre transmission tunnel. Fascia finished in vinyl treated fabric. Fitted carpet over floor. Seats trimmed with hide facings. Padded hide and vinyl treated fabric armrest between front bucket seats. Detachable side windows, having polished alloy frames with one fixed and one sliding perspex panel. Paint finish in single or dual colours.

Optional extras: Radio, Hardtop, Heater, Electrically operated overdrive. 15 × 4J wire spoke 'knock-on' wheels.

Leading Dimensions: Wheelbase 7 ft. 8 in. (2.336 m.); overall length 13 ft. 1½ in. (4.00 m.); overall height (hood up) 4 ft. 2 in. (1.244 m.); overall height (hood down) 3 ft. 10 in. (1.168 m.); overall width 5 ft. 0½ in. (1.536 m.); height over scuttle 2 ft. 11⅞ in. (0.914 m.); ground clearance 4½ in. (0.114 m.); track, front at ground level 4 ft. 0¾ in. (1.238 m.); track, rear 4 ft. 2 in. (1.270 m.); turning circle 35 ft. 0 in. (19.668 m.).

Vehicle weights: complete with tools, spare wheel, standard disc wheels, less fuel—2-seater 2,381 lb. (1,080 kg.); 4-seater 2,375 lb. (1,077 kg.). With tools, spare wheel, overdrive and wire wheels, less fuel—2-seater 2,408 lb. (1,092 kg.); 4-seater 2,393 lb. (1,085 kg.).

THE AUSTIN MOTOR COMPANY LIMITED
L O N G B R I D G E · · · B I R M I N G H A M

AUSTIN MOTOR EXPORT CORPORATION LIMITED
L O N G B R I D G E · B I R M I N G H A M · E N G L A N D

Printed in England

Publication No. 1733

In the beginning the motor of the Austin Healey, bored out to almost three liters, produced 124 HP, stood out through its powerful elasticity, and had lost nothing of its reliability.

Austin Healey

3000

2-SEATER AND OCCASIONAL 4-SEATER

SPORTS CARS

UOJ 412

In 1960 there appeared an inclusive catalog
for the 3000; its title page, looking quite
nostalgic today, is to be seen here.

GRACE AND PERFORMANCE

Sleek, smart and aerodynamic, the lines of the Austin Healey "3000" are pleasing to the eye, and it is available either as a two-seater or occasional four-seater sports tourer.

The remarkably ingenious design of the Austin Healey "3000" puts a 100 m.p.h. plus performance at your disposal and you will marvel at the way she holds the road, hugs the corners and eats up distance with effortless ease.

A classic example of British engineering at its best, this car will blaze a high speed trail of popularity along the highways of the world.

Included in the comprehensive all-weather equipment of the two- and four-seater Austin Healey "3000" is a tough vinyl treated fabric hood which can be speedily erected or folded away as necessary. Also provided is a tonneau cover of similar material which can be opened for driver only, or for driver and passenger, until it can be completely removed and stowed away in its specially designed wallet.

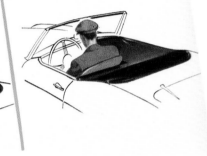

THE "3000" OCCASIONAL FOUR-SEATER 4

Each of the two front seats are adjustable. The seat cushions are removable and the squabs tilt forward to facilitate access to the inset well-type rear seats. An ash tray is provided in the centre transmission tunnel.

On the four-seater the spare wheel and battery are stowed in the rear boot and on both two- and four-seater cars a master switch operates from inside the compartment which has a lockable lid enabling the car to be safely left unattended.

In nice color pictures the advantages of the car are stressed, and many a woman also was taken by the British charm of this rawboned car.

The Austin Healey "3000" occasional four-seater is good to look at in its dual-tone paint finish, the smooth clean body lines presenting a delightfully pleasing picture from all points of view. Mechanically the four-seater is identical to its two-seater counterpart and is therefore still a sports car in the terms fullest meaning. The thrill of this type of motoring is now possible not only for you, but for three other members of the family also

Austin Healey

Each of the adjustable bucket seats in the neatly designed interior is upholstered in latex foam rubber, with hide facings. Two 6-volt batteries are contained in a locker beneath the spare wheel container. Gears are selected by a short central gear lever and for driving comfort the 17-inch diameter steering wheel has spring spokes. Each door has an open pocket for personal items, and a hard-wearing carpet over the entire floor completes the stylish interior trim.

2

THE "3000" TWO-SEATER SPORTS

The new two-seater "3000" is soundly designed from bumper to bumper. Power is transmitted through a four-speed synchromesh gearbox to the hypoid rear axle which carries ventilated pressed steel disc wheels fitted with 5.90—15 road speed tyres. A fine range of single or dual-tone colours is available and to suit individual needs there are numerous items of equipment such as heater, overdrive, and wire wheels which can be fitted at extra cost. But whatever the choice, the new "3000" cannot fail to be the centre of attraction and the subject of much favourable comment.

The spare wheel is stowed in a special container in the rear compartment leaving a surprising amount of space available for family luggage. Lighting equipment consists of powerful double-dipping headlamps, flashing direction indicators combined with sidelamps at front and stop/tail lamps at rear. A number plate illumination lamp is mounted in the rear bumper.

If the "occasional four-seater" was intended as an occasional family car, which corresponded very little to the nature of the car, the uncompromising two-seater still offered a more harmonious overall appearance.

41

For ease of entry, forward hinged doors open wide and the lower edges lift well clear of the kerb or sidewalk.

Aluminium framed side screens have one fixed and one sliding perspex panel for ventilation or hand signalling.

All instruments of the Austin Healey "3000" are easily readable, being closely grouped in a panel in front of the driver. On the opposite side of the trimmed fascia is a grab-handle for the convenience of the passenger. There is a parcel shelf beneath the fascia for motoring accessories, and the wide curved windscreen provides excellent vision ahead. A centrally placed driving mirror ensures that following traffic can be kept safely in view.

When a heater is required it can be neatly installed, the controls being fitted centrally as an integral part of the fascia.

THE B.M.C. 2·9 LITRE POWER UNIT

The power plant of the "3000" is a sturdy six cylinder overhead-valve unit of 2,912 c.c. capacity. It is fitted with twin HD6 semi-downdraught S.U. carburetters, and has already proved itself capable of sustained high speed motoring in excess of 100 m.p.h. Developing 124 b.h.p. at 4,600 r.p.m. (gross 130 b.h.p. at 4,750 r.p.m.) its smooth effortless power over long periods of very fast driving is delightful to experience.

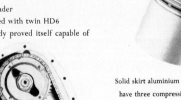

Solid skirt aluminium alloy pistons have three compression rings and one slotted oil control ring.

The timing chain is automatically adjusted by a slipper-type tensioner.

BRAKES

Large diameter hydraulic drum brakes are fitted on the rear wheels and 11¼″ (0.29 m.) diameter disc brakes on the front wheels ensure safe and progressive stopping power when travelling at the high speeds of which this car is capable.

SUSPENSION

Sturdy, independent front suspension units are controlled by hydraulic shock absorbers and stabilizing bar.
Rear suspension is by long semi-elliptic leaf springs. These are controlled by hydraulic shock absorbers and laterally stabilised by a panhard rod.

TRANSMISSION

The basic two or four-seater Austin Healey "3000" is equipped with a four speed gearbox which has synchromesh engagement on second, third and top speeds. All components are subjected to rigid scrutiny and testing before assembly to ensure maximum efficiency in operation. Power is transmitted to the three quarter floating hypoid rear axle by an open propeller shaft with needle roller universal joints.

OVERDRIVE

An electrically controlled overdrive (illustrated here) can, if required, be fitted to the standard gearbox of the Austin Healey "3000". This is operated by a switch on the fascia and provides a high top gear ratio giving the car a fast cruising speed, while maintaining a modest fuel consumption.

HEATER

For extremely cold climates, a fresh air heater with demisters can be neatly installed.

RADIO

If you like a radio in your car, there is a set available which gives good reception in all countries of the world.

The robust, four-bearing, fully-balanced crankshaft is fitted with an external vibration damper on its forward end to eliminate any whip at high revs.

OPTIONAL EXTRAS

A fully comprehensive range of optional extras and alternative equipment is available for the Austin Healey "3000". They can all be fitted to order, at extra cost.

HARDTOP

A removable hard-top instantly gives the appearance and convenience of a sports saloon.

Left: In the interior there had been no great changes over the years; the 3000 had still had snap-on side windows in the beginning, like the first model.

Now standard disc brakes on the front wheels provided even better deceleration, and a motor-sparing overdrive was available as an option at extra charge.

Der *Austin Healey* 3000 Convertible

Der 3000 Convertible

Die Schalensitze mit ihren abnehmbaren Sitzpolstern haben einen Schaumgummi-Kern und sind mit echtem englischen Leder bezogen. Wie bei jedem sportlichen Wagen kann man die Sitze einzeln verstellen und die Lehne - zum leichteren Zugang zu den rückwärtigen Sitzplätzen - nach vorne umlegen.

In den Getriebetunnel eingelassen, liegt handlich der Aschenbecher und zwischen den beiden Sitzen befindet sich eine breite, gepolsterte Armstütze. Ersatzrad und Batterie liegen geschützt und griffbereit im Kofferraum, der darüberhinaus auch noch viel Platz für Gepäck bietet. Der Batterie-Hauptschalter, mit welchem man den gesamten Stromkreislauf abschalten kann, bietet eine zusätzliche Diebstahlsicherung.

Die profilierte Karosserie des Austin Healey 3000 ist in der ganzen Welt zum Begriff für einen klassischen Sportwagen geworden. Ohne diese zeitlos schönen Linien zu verändern, ist der Wagen nunmehr mit einem soliden Vollkabriolett-Verdeck ausgestattet worden.

Dieser Wagen, dessen ruhmreiche Erfolge bei zahlreichen internationalen Wettbewerben immer wieder größte Beachtung finden, ist in seiner neuen Version nunmehr sehr viel bequemer und luxuriöser geworden. Der geschmeidige, großvolumige Motor hat auch bei größter Beanspruchung noch beachtliche Reserven, sodaß man mühelos die längsten Strecken bewältigt.

Das festeingebaute Faltdach, die gewölbte Windschutzscheibe und seitlichen Kurbelfenster werden jetzt auch diejenigen für dieses Fahrzeug begeistern, die sich bisher nicht mit der typisch englischen sportlichen Auslegung mit Steckfenstern und Roadsterverdeck anfreunden konnten.

Das dauerhafte, kunstlederne Faltdach und die Kurbelfenster können leicht und schnell bedient werden. Dadurch ist der CONVERTIBLE ein echter Allwetterwagen geworden. Eine zusätzliche Entlüftung läßt sich durch das einfache Entfernen der flexiblen Heckscheibe erreichen.

The profiled body of the Austin Healey 3000 has become a worldwide concept of a classic sports car. Without changing these timelessly beautiful lines, the car has now been fitted with a solid full-convertible top.

This car, whose renowned success in numerous international races always attracts great attention, has become much more comfortable and luxurious now in its new version. The efficient, large-volume motor still has considerable reserves under even the greatest pressure, so that one easily masters the longest trips.

The built-in folding top, the bowed windshield and cranked side windows will now inspire even those who until now could not feel comfortable with the typically English sporting furnishings of snap-on windows and roadster top.

The bucket seats with their removable upholstery have a foam rubber center and are covered with genuine English leather. As in every sporting car, the seats can be adjusted individually, and the seat backs fold forward—for easier access to the back seats.

Mounted in the driveshaft tunnel is the handy ash tray, and between the two seats is a wide, upholstered armrest. The spare wheel and battery are protected and near at hand in the luggage compartment, which also offers much space for luggage. The main battery switch, by which the entire electrical system can be turned off, offers additional security against theft.

The lasting imitation leather folding top and the cranked windows can be used quickly and easily. They make the CONVERTIBLE a genuine all-weather car. Additional ventilation can be attained by simply removing the flexible rear window.

Mark II and III were available only in 2+2 form, to the sorrow of fans of the old two-seater. The auxiliary seats in the rear were usually used as additional luggage space.

Gestern, heute und morgen hatte und hat diese Karosserie ihre gültige Schönheit. Mit seiner neuen Ausstattung wird der Austin Healey 3000 CONVERTIBLE nur noch als klassischer 2/2-Sitzer hergestellt. Die Kraftübertragung erfolgt über das robuste, gut abgestufte Viergang-Getriebe auf die hypoidverzahnte Hinterachse. Preß-stahlscheibenräder mit der 5.90 x 15 Spezialbereifung und die auf die jeweilige Innen-ausstattung abgestimmte Ein- oder Zweifarbenlackierung sind Teile der Normalausführung.

Yesterday, today and tomorrow, this body had and has its valid beauty. With its new equipment, the Austin Healey 3000 CONVERTIBLE is produced only as a classic 2+2-seater. Power transmission takes place via the robust, well-balanced four-speed gearbox to the hypoid-geared rear axle. Pressed-steel disc wheels with special 5.90 x 15 tires and one or two-tone finish to match any interior decor are included in standard production.

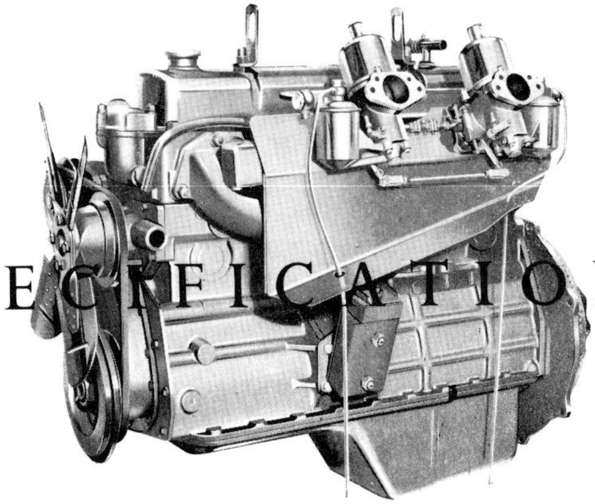

SPECIFICATION

ENGINE: 2,912 c.c. (177.7 cu. in.); bore 3.282 in. (83.36 mm.); stroke 3.5 in. (89 mm.); b.h.p. 124 at 4,600 r.p.m. (nett); 130 b.h.p. at 4,750 r.p.m. (gross); maximum torque 175 lb. ft. at 3,000 r.p.m.; compression ratio 9.03 to 1.
Cylinders: Six cylinders cast integral with crankcase.
Cylinder Head: Detachable in cast-iron with separate six-port cast aluminium inlet manifold. Two-piece cast-iron exhaust manifold fitted with twin exhaust system.
Crankshaft: Forged steel support by four steel-backed white metal bearings.
Connecting Rods: Forged steel with steel backed white metal bearings.
Pistons: Solid skirt, flat top pistons in aluminium alloy with tin-plated finish. Three compression rings and one slotted oil control ring fitted.
Camshaft: Forged steel in four steel-backed white metal bearings. Cams of patented design to give efficient and quiet operation. The camshaft gear is driven by duplex roller chain which has an integral oil feed and an automatic slipper type tensioner to maintain chain lubrication and tightness respectively.
Valves: Overhead, operated by push-rods and designed for silent operation. Valve oil seals are fitted. KE965 steel exhaust valves.
Lubrication: Oil is forced under pressure to all main, connecting rod and camshaft bearings and to each tappet. It is also fed to the timing chain and overhead valve rocker gear. The connecting rods have jet holes to provide oil for cylinder walls when starting-up. Both main and connecting rod oil feeds are of patented design to ensure longer crankshaft life. A full-flow oil filter is fitted, which has a renewable element. Oil capacity approximately 12 pints (6.8 litres).
Cooling: Circulation by fan and centrifugal pump with thermostat control. Water is delivered to the cylinder block and thence to ample passages surrounding the valve pockets and sparking plugs. A 4-bladed fan is fitted to export models. Cooling system capacity approximately 20 pints (11.37 litres).
Ignition: Coil and 12-volt battery. Automatic advance and retard and built-in vacuum control.
Fuel System: Fuel from a rear tank is fed by electric pump to two semi-downdraught S.U. HD6 carburetters fitted with "pancake" air cleaners. A stop tap is provided on the fuel tank. Tank capacity 12 gallons (54.6 litres).

CHASSIS: Transmission:

Clutch: Single dry plate, 10 in. (0.25 m.) diameter.

Gearbox: Ratios: Reverse 3.78; First 2.93; Second 2.053; Third 1.309; Top 1.0 to 1. Oil Capacity: approximately 4 pints (2.27 litres). Change speed: short central lever on floor.

Propeller Shaft: Open, with needle roller bearing universal joints.

Rear Axle: Ratio: 3.545 to 1 (11/39). Oil Capacity: approximately 3 pints (1.7 litres).

Road Speeds at 1,000 r.p.m.: First 7.15 m.p.h.; Second 10.2 m.p.h. Third 16.0 m.p.h.; Top 20.9 m.p.h.

Transmission with Overdrive:

Clutch: Single dry plate, 10 in. (0.25 m.) diameter.

Gearbox: Ratios—Reverse 3.78; First 2.93; Second 2.053; Third 1.309; Overdrive Third 1.076; Top 1.0 to 1; Overdrive Top 0.822. Change speed; short central lever on floor. Oil capacity: approximately 5½ pints (2.98 litres), including overdrive.

Propeller Shaft: Open, with needle roller bearing universal joints.

Rear Axle: Ratio, with overdrive: 3.91 to 1 (11/43). Oil capacity: approximately 3 pints (1.7 litres).

Road Speeds at 1,000 r.p.m.: First 6.475 m.p.h.; Second 9.24 m.p.h.; Third 14.47 m.p.h.; Overdrive Third 17.65 m.p.h.; Top 18.94 m.p.h.; Overdrive Top 23.1 m.p.h.

Steering: Cam and Peg. Ratio: 14 to 1. Steering Wheel: three spring spokes, 17 in. (0.43 m.) diameter.

Suspension: Front—Independent wishbones, coil springs, shock absorbers and stabilizing bar Rear—Semi-elliptic leaf springs, shock absorbers and panhard rod. Hydraulic lever type, shock absorbers.

Brakes: Girling hydraulic. 11¼ in. (0.29 m.) discs on front. Drum type 11 in. diameter × 2¼ in. wide on rear.

Road Wheels: 15 in. × 4J, Ventilated Steel Disc. Fixing: 5 nuts. Tyres: 5.90—15 Road Speed.

Electrical: 12 volt (consisting of two 6 volt batteries on 2-seater), 50 ampere hour capacity at 10 hour rate, (57 ampere hour at 20 hour rate). Headlamps with dipping switch and equipment to suit regulations of different countries. Combined side lamps and flashing direction indicators. Combined twin stop-tail lamps and flashing direction indicators. Concealed instrument panel lamps. Twin horns. Twin windscreen wipers.

Instruments: Trip speedometer. Revolution counter. Fuel gauge. Combined water temperature and oil pressure gauge. Red warning lights indicate no dynamo charge and headlamp high beam position. Green warning light shows direction indicators working. Switches for starter, lighting, screen wiper, and control for windscreen washer (also for heater and overdrive when fitted) on instrument panel. Panel light switch on lower edge of fascia. Windscreen washer.

Coachwork: Two or four-seater, two-door, open sports tourer with all-weather protection. Steel/aluminium construction. Bonnet top—with chrome grille vent to assist engine cooling—hinged at rear edge and supported in open position by a pivoted rod. Bonnet lock operated from inside car. Wide rear-opening doors fitted with outside handles. A large open pocket is provided in each door. Fixed curved windscreen of laminated plate glass fitted with double screen wipers. Folding hood of vinyl treated fabric includes large transparent backlight which—with hood sticks—can be completely removed. A tonneau cover completely covers seats but can be opened for driver only. Luggage compartment with lockable lid at rear, lined with Armacord and containing spare wheel in special container over rear axle on two-seater, on floor of boot in four-seater. Front and rear chrome bumpers with overriders. Twin rear reflectors. Adjustable front bucket seats, the squabs of which tilt forward to give access to the rear compartment. Batteries in special locker beneath spare wheel container on two-seater and in luggage boot on four-seater. Master switch independently operated from inside luggage compartment. All instruments grouped on driver's side of fascia, grab handle on passenger side. Interior driving mirror and trimmed crash pad fitted to top of scuttle, behind windscreen. Parcel tray fitted below fascia. Flush fitting ash tray in centre transmission tunnel. Fascia finished in vinyl treated fabric. Fitted carpet over floor. Seats trimmed with hide facings. Padded hide and vinyl treated fabric armrest between front bucket seats. Detachable side windows having polished alloy frames with one fixed and one sliding perspex panel. Paint finish in single or dual colours.

Optional extras: Radio, Hardtop. Heater. Electrically operated overdrive 15 in. × 4J wire spoke 'knock-on' wheels.

Leading Dimensions: Wheelbase 7 ft. 8 in. (2.336 m.); overall length 13 ft. 1½ in. (4.00 m.); overall height (hood up) 4 ft. 2 in. (1.244 m.); overall height (hood down) 3 ft. 10 in. (1.168 m.); overall width 5 ft. 0½ in. (1.536 m.); height over scuttle 2 ft. 11⅞ in. (0.914 m.); ground clearance 4½ in. (0.114 m.); track, front at ground level 4 ft. 0¾ in. (1.238 m.); track, rear 4 ft. 2 in. (1.270 m.); turning circle 35 ft. 0 in. (19.668 m.).

Vehicle weights: complete with tools, spare wheel, standard disc wheels. less fuel—2-seater 2381 lb. (1080 kg.); 4-seater 2375 lb. (1077 kg.), With tools, spare wheel, overdrive and wire wheels, less fuel—2-seater 2408 lb. (1092 kg.); 4-seater 2393 lb. (1085 kg.).

THE AUSTIN MOTOR COMPANY LIMITED
LONGBRIDGE. . BIRMINGHAM

AUSTIN MOTOR EXPORT CORPORATION LIMITED
LONGBRIDGE . BIRMINGHAM . ENGLAND

Printed in England

Publication No. 1734

The technical data in the original English catalog of 1960.

The sales catalogs of the successor Mark II and III types differ only in the lettering of the title page and a few passages in the text.

For these last two versions of the big Austin Healey it had been decided to have the bars of the radiator grille run vertically.

47

Durch die seitlich herumgezogene Windschutzsche
ohnehin ausgezeichnete Sicht nach vorne no
Scheibenwaschanlage und weitreichende, sich
anpassende Scheibenwischer halten die Sicht au
Wetter

Die vorn angeschlagenen
Türen öffnen sich weit
und hoch genug über
der Bordsteinkante zum
bequemen Ein- und
Aussteigen.

Bemerkenswerte Punkte des

Wenn notwendig, dann bietet der Austi
Healey 3000 den Komfort und die Cl
borgenheit einer Limousine. Bei gute
Wetter aber verwandelt man den Wa
mit wenigen Handgriffen in einen ech
Roadster. Durch den leicht gängigen
durchdachten Mechanismus ist das Ö
oder Schließen des Faltdaches eine
fache Angelegenheit auch für Dame

Not for purists, but otherwise of inestimable value, was the installation of cranked windows in the last two versions, which, along with small vent windows, made ventilating the interior much more controllable. Comfort above all for American customers!

lealey CONVERTIBLE

In the Mark II, a fully new dashboard design with wood veneer provided a luxurious atmosphere, and a folding rear seat allowed American housewives to stow the weekly groceries themselves without problems . . .

The vehicles produced by the Austin Motor Company Limited have a guarantee that makes all other guarantees, conditions, legal and other conditions superfluous. The right to make technical and other changes at any time—with or without announcement—is reserved.

Austin Motor Company Ltd., Longbridge, Birmingham/England

Austin Motor Export Corporation Ltd.

Longbridge, Birmingham/England

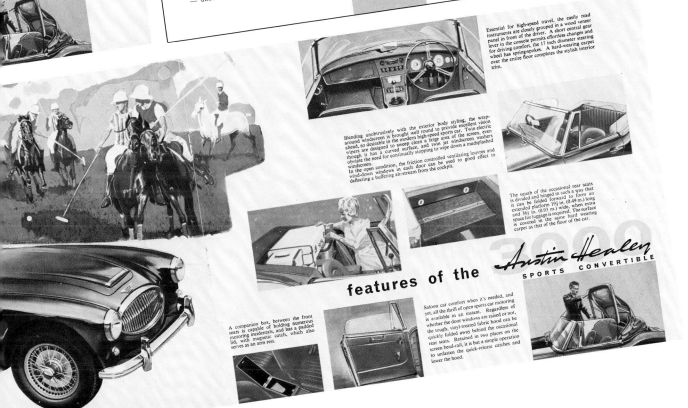

Essential for high-speed travel, the easily read instruments are closely grouped in a wood veneer panel in front of the driver. A short central gear lever in the console permits effortless changes and for driving comfort, the 17 inch diameter steering wheel has spring-spokes. A hard-wearing carpet over the entire floor completes the stylish interior trim.

Blending unobtrusively with the exterior body styling, the wrap-around windscreen is brought well round to provide excellent vision ahead, so desirable in the modern high-speed sports car. Twin electric wipers are designed to sweep clean a large area of the screen, even though it has a curved surface, and twin jet windscreen washers obviate the need for continually stopping to wipe down a mudsplashed windscreen.
In the open condition, the friction controlled ventilating louvres and wind-down windows in each door can be used to good effect in deflecting a buffeting air-stream from the cockpit.

The squab of the occasional rear seats is divided and hinged in such a way that it can be folded forward to form an extended platform 19¼ in. (0.49 m.) long and 36½ in. (0.93 m.) wide, when extra space for luggage is required. The surface is covered in the same hard wearing carpet as that of the floor of the car.

features of the *Austin Healey* **3000 SPORTS CONVERTIBLE**

A companion box, between the front seats is capable of holding numerous motoring incidentals, and has a padded lid, with magnetic catch, which also serves as an arm rest.

Saloon car comfort when it's needed, and yet, all the thrill of open sports car motoring is available in an instant. Regardless of whether the door windows are raised or not, the tough, vinyl-treated fabric hood can be quickly folded away behind the occasional rear seats. Retained in two places on the screen head-rail, it is but a simple operation to unfasten the quick-release catches and lower the hood.

Das Herz des Austin Healey 3000 Mk II ist der berühmte
2,9 Liter 6-Zylinder-BMC-Motor mit 2 HS6-Halbstrom-SU-
Vergasern. Der Ölumlauf wird durch einen Auswechselfilter
im Hauptstrom sauber gehalten. Diese robuste Maschine ent-
wickelt bei 4750 U/min. 130 PS. Seit Jahren ist dieser Motor
bekannt durch seine Leistung, Elastizität und Lebensdauer.
Unempfindlichkeit gegen Dauergeschwindigkeiten und große
Kraftreserve am Berg haben dem Austin Healey 3000 immer
zu seinen aufsehenerregenden Erfolgen auf den bekannten,
internationalen Langstrecken-Wettbewerben verholfen.

Der BMC 2·9 -Liter-Motor

Die stabile, vierfachgelagerte, elektrisch ausgewuchtete
Kurbelwelle ist zur Vermeidung von Vibrationsschwin-
gungen bei hohen Drehzahlen vorne mit einem
Schwingungsdämpfer versehen.

The power plant of the 3000 is a sturdy six-cylinder overhead-valve unit of
2,912 c.c. capacity. It is fitted with two HD 8 semi-down draught S.U. carburetters and its oil circulation is protected by a full-flow oil filter which traps all
damaging foreign bodies in a replaceable element. Developing 150 b.h.p. at
5,250 r.p.m., this long-lasting engine has already proved itself capable of sustained
high-speed motoring in excess of 100 m.p.h. Its smooth, effortless power over
long periods of very fast driving is delightfully exhilarating to experience and its
lively response through the gears gives to the Austin Healey 3000 Sports
Convertible the magnificent sports car performance it deserves!

The BMC 2·9 litre power unit

The robust, four-bearing, fully-balanced
crankshaft is fitted with an external
vibration damper on its forward end to
eliminate any whip at high revs.

ge-dimensioned hydraulic Girling brake system with 29-cm
r disc brakes in front and 27.94 x 5.72-cm brake drums in the
is ideally balanced combination of brakes gives the car
m braking values.
ion
stable independent suspension with hydraulic shock absorbers
ilizer. In back a rigid axle on long half-elliptic leaf springs
lraulic shock absorbers and stabilizer.

ıdard gearbox is a four-speed type, which is synchronized in
third and fourth gears.—The greatest possible care in
ture and assembly guarantee easy working and great operating
he power transmission takes place via the hypoid-geared rear
the driveshaft with needle-bearing cross links.
L EQUIPMENT
ossibilities for fulfilling extra wishes for the Austin Healey
ʰNVERTIBLE.
r heating: Easy to regulate and capable enough even in the
weather; likewise formed as a windshield defroster. In the
ıodel the heater is part of the standard equipment.

nercially available auto radios can be built in.
wheels:
ıdard model is equipped with pressed-steel disc wheels. To
the roadholding and provide greater cooling for the brakes,
drivers can optionally obtain spoked wheels.
overdrive: Provides two additional degrees of gearing in third
ʰ gears. With overdrive switched on, the result is a reduction
e speed by about 20%, which spares engine wear and reduces
sumption.

Bremsen

Die großdimensionierte hydraulische
Girling-Bremsanlage mit 29 cm ⌀
Scheibenbremsen vorn und 27,94 x
5,72 cm Trommelbremsen hinten –
diese vorzüglich abgestimmte Brems-
kombination verschafft dem Wagen
maximale Verzögerungswerte.

Aufhängung

Vorne stabile Einzelradaufhängung
mit hydraulischen Hebelstoßdämpfern
und Stabilisator.
Hinten Starrachse an langen, halb-
elliptischen Blattfedern mit hydraulischen Stoßdämpfern und
Stabilisator.

Das serienmäßige Getriebe ist ein Vierganggetriebe, welches im zweiten,
dritten und vierten Gang synchronisiert ist. – Größtmögliche Sorgfalt bei
der Herstellung und Montage garantieren leichte Funktion und große
Betriebssicherheit. Die Kraftübertragung erfolgt auf die hypoidverzahnte
Hinterachse über die Gelenkwelle mit Nadellager-Kreuzgelenken.

SONDERZUBEHÖR

Einige Möglichkeiten zur Erfüllung von Extrawünschen
für den Austin Healey 3000 CONVERTIBLE.

Frischluftheizung: Gut regelbar und auch
beikältestem Wetter leistungsfähig genug;
gleichzeitig als Scheibendefroster ausgebildet. Im Exportmodell gehört diese
Heizung zur serienmäßigen Ausstattung.

Radio

Alle im Handel erhältlichen
Autoempfänger lassen sich
einbauen.

Speichenräder:
Das Standard-Modell ist mit
Preßstahlscheibenrädern aus-
gerüstet. Zur Vervollkommnung
der Straßenlage und größeren
Kühlung der Bremsen können
sportliche Fahrer auf Wunsch
Speichenräder mit Zentral-
verschluß bekommen.

Elektrischer Overdrive: Schafft zwei zusätzliche
Getriebeabstufungen im dritten und vierten Gang.
Bei eingeschaltetem Overdrive ergibt sich eine
etwa 20%ige Drehzahlverringerung und bewirkt
Motorschonung und Kraftstoffersparnis.

**More effective carburetors, a sharper camshaft and
the reworking of the fuel inlets helped the Mark
III motor attain approximately 150 HP, which
allowed the roadster to exceed the 200-kph mark.**

Export-Ausführung

Wahlweise ohne Aufpreis

Rechts- oder Linkslenkung; Meilen- oder Kilometer-zähler; 4- oder 6-Flügelventilator.

Sonderzubehör (gegen Berechnung)

Verstellbare Lenksäule, Zigarren-Anzünder, zwei Außenspiegel, Overdrive, Nebellampe und Such-scheinwerfer, abschließbarer Tankverschluß, Speichen-räder, Servo-Bremshilfe, Gepäckständer und Radio.

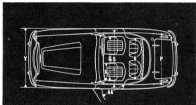

TECHNISCHE DATEN

MOTOR: Hubraum: 2912 ccm, Bohrung 83,36 mm, Hub 89 mm, PS 130 bei 4750 U/min, Drehmoment maximal 23,15 m/kg bei 3000 U/min, Verdichtung 9,03:1.

Zylinder: Sechszylinder.

Zylinderkopf: abnehmbar, mit drei separaten Aluminium-Ansaugkrümmern; zweiteiliger, gußeiserner Auspuffkrümmer mit Zwillings-Auspuffanlage.

Kurbelwelle: Schmiedestahl, vierfach gelagert in stahlverstärkten Weißmetallagern.

Pleuel: Schmiedestahl mit stahlverstärkten Weißmetallagern.

Kolben: Zinnverstärkte Aluminium-Flachbodenkolben mit drei Kompressionsringen und einem Olabstreifring.

Nockenwelle: Schmiedestahl; vierfach gelagert in verstärkten Weißmetallagern, mit Patenthochleistungsnocken, die ruhigen Lauf gewährleisten. Duplex-Rollensteuerketten-Antrieb mit eingebauter Olzufuhr und selbsttätigem Spanner mit Dämpfer.

Ventile: obengesteuert, durch Stößel betätigt, geräuscharme Konstruktion; alle Ventilschächte mit Dichtungsringen; KE 965 Spezial-Auslaßventile.

Schmierung: Oldruckschmierung aller Haupt-, Pleuel-, Nockenwellenlager, Stößelstangen, der Nockenwellenantriebskette und des gesamten Zylinderkopfes; Kurbelwelle mit längerer Lebensdauer durch patentierte Haupt- und Pleuellager-Olzufuhr; eingebauter Hauptstrom-Olfilter mit Auswechsel-element; Olwannenkapazität ungefähr 6,8 Liter.

Kühlung: eingebauter Vierflügel-Ventilator und Kreiselpumpe, thermostatisch gesteuert. Das Wasser wird über den Zylinderblock in die Kanäle geleitet, von denen die Ventilsitze und Zündkerzen umgeben sind; 11,37-Liter-Kühltank.

Zündung: 12-Volt-Batterie und Zündspule, eingebaute Vakuumkontrolle.

Treibstoffzufuhr: Vom 54,6-Liter-Hecktank zum Halbfallstrom-SU-Doppelvergaser HS6, mit Trockenluftfilter.

CHASSIS: Kraftübertragung:

Kupplung: 25 cm ⌀ Einscheibentrockenkupplung.

Getriebe: Übersetzungen: Rückwärtsgang 3,78; erster 2,93; zweiter 2,053; dritter 1,309; vierter 1,0:1. Olkapazität etwa 2,27 Liter.

Schaltung: direkt mittels zentralem, sportlich kurzem Schaltstock.

Gelenkwelle: offen, mit Nadellager-Kreuzgelenken.

Hinterachse: Übersetzung 3,545:1 (11/39) – Olkapazität etwa 1,7 Liter.

Geschwindigkeiten bei 1000 U/min: Erster Gang 11,45; zweiter 17,25; dritter 25,6; vierter 33,44 km/h.

Getriebe mit Overdrive

Kupplung: Einscheiben-Trockenkupplung 25 cm ⌀.

Getriebe: Abstufung: Rückwärtsgang 3,78; erster Gang 2,93; zweiter 2,053; dritter 1,309 - mit Overdrive 1,076; vierter 1,0 : 1 - mit Overdrive 0,822.

Schaltung: direkt mittels zentralem, sportlich kurzem Schaltstock.

Gelenkwelle: offen, mit Nadellager-Kreuzgelenken.

Hinterachse: Übersetzung mit Overdrive 3,91:1 (11/43) - Olkapazität ca. 1,7 Liter.

Geschwindigkeiten bei 1000 U/min: erster Gang 10,35; zweiter 14,8; dritter 23,15 - mit Overdrive 28,25; vierter 30,3 - mit Overdrive 37 km/h.

Lenkung: Schnecke und Segment, 14:1 übersetzt: Dreifederspeichen-Lenkrad 43 cm ⌀.

Aufhängung: vorne - Einzelradaufhängung mit Dreieckslenkern, Schrau-benfedern, Stoßdämpfern, Stabilisator. Hinten - halbelliptische Blatt-federn, Panhardstab und hydraulische Hebelstoßdämpfer.

Bremsen: Fußbremse: hydraulische Girling-Anlage; vorne - Scheiben-bremsen 29 cm ⌀; hinten - Trommelbremsen 27,94 x 5,72 cm; Handbremse wirkt mechanisch auf die Hinterräder.

Räder: Preßstahlscheibenräder 15x4J mit Ventilationsschlitzen, 5-Bolzen-Befestigung; Bereifung 5,90 x 15.

Elektrische Ausrüstung: 12-Volt-Batterie mit 50/10 oder 57/20 amp/h; Scheinwerfer mit Fuß-Abblendschalter; Seitenlampen mit Frontblinkern, Brems- und Schlußleuchten mit Heckblinkern kombiniert; blendfreie Instrumentenbeleuchtung; Zweiklanghorn; 2 Scheibenwischer.

Instrumente: Tageszähler, Drehzahlmesser, Benzinuhr, Fernthermometer mit Oldruckmesser, Kontrollampen für Lichtmaschine, Fernlicht und Blinker; Schalter für Anlasser, Beleuchtung, Scheibenwischer. Scheibenwaschanlage, Heizung und Overdrive; Instrumentenbeleuch-tungsschalter an der Armaturenbrett-Unterkante.

TECHNICAL DATA
(Information identical to that given in English on page 46. Box at right:)
MEASUREMENTS
(Bodenfreiheit ') Ground clearance
Turning circle: 10.67 m. Front track: 1.24 m.
Weight: 1077 kg Rear track: 1.27 m.

ABMESSUNGEN

A	C	E	G	J
0,89 m	0,50 m	0,51 m	0,21 m	0,49 m
K	**L**	**N**	**O**	**P**
0,14 m	1,22 m	0,36 m	0,72 m	0,21 m
Q1	**Q2**	**R**	**S**	**W**
0,43 m	1,14 m	0,99 m	1,28 m	2,34 m
X	**Y**	**Z**	**AA**	**Boden-freiheit**
1,24 m	1,54 m	4,00 m	0,67 m	0,11 m

Wendekreis 10,67 m	Spur vorne : 1,24 m
Gewicht 1077 kg	Spur hinten : 1,27 m

Karosserie: 2/2 Sitzer, zweitüriges Stahl-Aluminium-Kabriolett, auf Wunsch zweifarbig. Oben eingehängte Motorhaube mit Aufstellstange und verchromten Luftschlitzen im Kühlergrill. Motorhaube wird vom Wageninneren aus betätigt; doppelter Sicherheitsriegel. Breite, vorn angeschlagene, weit öffnende Türen mit Außengriffen, Kurbel- und Ausstellfenstern, sowie geräumige Türtaschen. Feststehende, gewölbte Windschutzscheibe mit zwei Scheibenwischern und Halterungen für die Knebel des Kunstleder-Faltdaches, das aufgrund seiner Verdecksschere leicht vor- und zurückklappbar ist. Der mit Armacord ausgekleidete, verschließbare Kofferraum enthält die Batterie nebst Hauptschalter und das verankerte Ersatzrad. Alle Skalen und Bedienungselemente sind übersichtlich bzw. handlich vor dem Fahrer angeordnet; Beifahrer-Haltegriff, Innenspiegel mit Anti-Reflex-Belag auf der gepolsterten Armaturenbrett-Oberkante; offenes Ablagefach über dem vorderen Beinraum; versenkbarer Aschenbecher auf dem Getriebetunnel; maßge-rechter Velours-Bodenbelag; lederbezogene Sitze, gepolsterte Armstütze zwischen den einzeln verstellbaren Front-Schalensitzen mit Kipplehnen für die besseren Zugang zum Fond, Stoßstange mit Zierhörnern verchromt.

Sonderzubehör: Radio, elektrischer Overdrive, 15 x 4 J Speichenräder, Servo-Bremsanlage; Sitzabdeckung (auf der Fahrerseite rückklappbar) passend zum Faltdach.

Excerpt from the special brochure of the Austin importer
Brüggemann in Düsseldorf. The Sprite cost only half as much as the
3000.

An automobile program that fulfills all wishes and suits every need!

In this catalog you will find the cars of the Austin Group. From lively little sports cars to big, impressive sedans, everything is there that will make a motorist's heart beat faster. All cars of the Austin Group have one thing in common: They are unconditionally dedicated to quality. This fact finds expression in the guarantee that one might describe as absolutely unusual: It covers a whole year without regard for the distance driven, without looking at the number of kilometers. How good does a car from Austin have to be if such an achievement is offered freely! Austin has built good cars for over fifty years. United with the Nuffield Group to form BMC, this firm belongs to the five most significant automobile manufacturers in the world. Every vehicle that leaves the big factory is a good example of the perfection of workmanship and technology of English motor vehicle construction and makes sure that the name of Austin is spoken with true enthusiasm everywhere. Drive an Austin—enjoy the pleasure of an automobile in its highest potency! Whoever drives an Austin knows the satisfying driving experience that unites all Austin drivers . . .

Ein automobilistisches Programm, das alle Wünsche erfüllt und jedem Bedarf gerecht wird!

Sie finden in diesem Prospekt die Wagen der Austin-Gruppe. Vom kleinen, wendigen Sportwagen bis zur großen, repräsentativen Limousine ist alles da, was das Herz eines Autofahrers höher schlagen läßt. Alle Wagen der Austin-Gruppe haben eins gemeinsam: Sie bekennen sich bedingungslos zur Qualität. Diese Tatsache findet Ausdruck in der Garantie, die man als absolut ungewöhnlich bezeichnen möchte: sie erstreckt sich ohne Rücksicht auf die gefahrene Strecke, ohne Rücksicht auf die Kilometerzahl auf ein ganzes Jahr! Wie gut muß doch ein Wagen von Austin sein, wenn eine solche Leistung aus freien Stücken geboten wird! Austin baut seit über 50 Jahren gute Automobile. Mit der Nuffield-Gruppe vereint zur BMC, gehört dieses Unternehmen zu den fünf bedeutendsten Automobil-Produzenten der Welt. Jedes Fahrzeug, welches das große Werk verläßt, ist ein markantes Beispiel für die handwerkliche und technische Vollkommenheit des englischen Kraftwagenbaus und sorgt dafür, daß der Name Austin überall mit echter Begeisterung ausgesprochen wird. Fahren Sie Austin — genießen Sie die Freude am Automobil in höchster Potenz! Wer einen Austin fährt, kennt das beglückende Fahr-Erlebnis, das alle Austin-Fahrer verbindet . . .

A big-class sports car! One of the fastest on all roads, inspiringly beautiful in its thoroughbred form. Convincing in its performance! The 2.912-liter motor—producing 130 SAE HP—gives the car a power to move that lets you master every situation. The disc brakes bring it to a stop in no time. Its roadholding is the basis of its safety—you trust the 3000, even at its top speed!

The buyer can choose between the classic two-seater roadster and the +2-seat car that can carry four people. In this form the 3000 presents itself as a "family" sports car! Let it introduce itself to you soon! When you have seen and driven it, then your decision is firm: for you too, here is just one full-blooded sports car of the great English class!

AUSTIN-HEALEY „3000"

2912 ccm | PS 130 | 12 L | 2/2 | 12900,—

Ein Sportwagen der großen Klasse! Einer der schnellsten auf allen Straßen, begeisternd schön in seiner rassigen Form. Überzeugend in seiner Leistung! Der 2.912-Liter-Motor — Leistung 130 SAE-PS — verleiht dem Wagen eine Kraft des Anzuges, die Sie jede Situation meistern läßt. Die Scheibenbremsen bringen ihn im Nu zum Stehen. Seine Straßenlage ist das Unterpfand Ihrer Sicherheit — Sie vertrauen dem 3000 auch bei höchstem Tempo!
Der Käufer hat die Wahl zwischen dem klassischen zweisitzigen Roadster und dem Wagen mit 2/2 Sitzen, in dem sich vier Personen befördern lassen. In dieser Form präsentiert sich der 3000 als ,familiengerechter' Sportwagen! Lassen Sie sich bald vorführen! Wenn Sie ihn gesehen und gefahren haben, dann steht Ihr Entschluß fest: auch für Sie gibt es dann nur einen Vollblut-Sportwagen der großen englischen Klasse!

Everyone who likes to sit behind the wheel of their car with enthusiasm dreams of a sports car. The Austin Healey Sprite makes his wish fulfillable: finally a sports car that is affordable! Finally a fast, nimble, racy car that proves itself again and again in the daily test of city traffic with its quick starting, often giving you the advantage that sets you apart from others in that traffic! The Sprite has bucket seats that fit the body. A sports car of English quality—unbeaten in its class! Direct steering, low center of gravity, deliberate limitation to the necessities—one plus after another.

Since the Sprite exists, scarcely anyone has to do without that "sports-car feeling" any more! Sit down in one! Give it gas! The powerful sound of the motor will make you happy!

AUSTIN-HEALEY SPRITE

948 ccm | PS 42,5 | 7,5 L | 2 | 6990,—

Von einem Sportwagen träumen alle, die sich mit Begeisterung hinter das Lenkrad ihres Wagens setzen. Der Austin Healy Sprite macht diesen Wunsch erfüllbar: endlich ein Sportwagen der erschwinglich ist! Endlich ein schnelles, wendiges, rasantes Fahrzeug, das sich in der täglichen Praxis des Stadtverkehrs durch sprunghaftes Startvermögen immer wieder neu bewährt und Ihnen dadurch oft den Vorsprung bietet, auf den es Ihnen im Vergleich zu anderen Verkehrsteilnehmern ankommt! Der Sprite hat körpergerechte Schalensitze. Ein Sportwagen englischer Prägung — in seiner Klasse unübertroffen! Direkte Lenkung, niedrige Schwerpunktlage, zweckmäßige Beschränkung auf das Notwendige — so kommt ein Pluspunkt zum anderen.
Seitdem es den Sprite gibt, braucht kaum jemand mehr auf das „Sportscar-Feeling" zu verzichten! Setzen Sie sich hinein! Geben Sie Gas! Das kraftvolle Geräusch des Motors wird Sie glücklich stimmen!

The ideal sport two-seater
AUSTIN HEALEY "Sprite"
TECHNICAL DESCRIPTION

Motor: 4-cylinder in-line motor, overhead camshaft, balanced crankshaft with three main bearings. Bore 62.9 mm, stroke 76.2 mm, displacement 948 cc. 43 HP at 5000 rpm, highest allowable engine speed 6000 rpm, compression ratio 8.3:1.

Fuel system: 2 H-1 inclined downdraft SU carburetors, mechanical A.C. Type Y fuel pump. 2 flat oil-bath air filters. Capacity of the fuel tank 28 liters.

Lubrication: Mainstream pressure lubrication. Geared or vaned oil pump, driven by the camshaft. Changeable mainstream oil filter mounted outside. Oil capacity of the sump 3.5 liters, plus 0.6 liter for the filter.

Ignition: Pressure-regulated automatic distributor.

Cooling: Pressure cooling with pump, ventilator and thermostat. Radiator capacity approximately 6 liters.

Clutch: Single-plate dry clutch, diameter 16 cm, hydraulically activated.

Gears: Four speeds, synchronized in second, third and fourth. Gear ratios: 1st gear 3.628, 2nd gear 2.734, 3rd gear 1.412, 4th gear 1.000, reverse 4.664. Centrally mounted gearshift lever. Gearbox oil capacity approximately 1.4 liters.

Driveshaft: Open, with needle roller bearings. Sliding wedges in the gearbox.

Rear axle: Hypoid, three-quarter swinging, banjo-type. Final drive ratio 4.22:1 (9/38). Oil capacity approximately 1 liter.

Total gear ratios: 1st gear 15.31, 2nd gear 10.02, 3rd gear 5.96, 4th gear 4.22, reverse 19.68.

Speeds at 1000 rpm: 1st gear 6.7 kph, 2nd gear 10.3 kph, 3rd gear 17.4 kph, 4th gear 24.6 kph.

Steering: Rack-and-pinion steering, 2.33 (two and one-third) turns from block to block. Two-spoked steering wheel, diameter 41 cm. Turning circle approximately 9.60 meters.

Suspension: Independent front suspension with radius arms, coil springs and shock absorbers. Rear quarter-elliptic leaf springs with shock absorbers and radius arms. Hydraulic lever shock absorbers.

Brakes: Hydraulic foot brakes acting on all four wheels. Two front brake shoes. Hand brake acting on rear wheels via compensator, centrally mounted. Diameter 17.50 x 3.5 cm.

Der ideale Sportzweisitzer.

AUSTIN HEALEY »Sprite«

TECHNISCHE BESCHREIBUNG

Motor: 4 Zylinder, Reihenmotor, obengesteuert, wassergekühlt, dreifach gelagerte und ausgewuchtete Kurbelwelle, Bohrung 62.9 mm, Hub 76.2 mm, Kubikinhalt 948 ccm. 43 PS bei 5000 U/min, höchstzulässige Drehzahl 6000 U/min. Verdichtungsverhältnis 8.3 : 1.

Treibstoffsystem: 2 H 1-Schrägfallstrom-SU-Vergaser. Mechanische A.C.-Benzinpumpe der Type Y. 2 flache Öl-Luftfilter. Fassungsraum des Benzintanks 28 Liter.

Schmierung: Hauptstrom-Druckumlaufschmierung, Zahnrad- oder Flügel-Ölpumpe, von der Nockenwelle angetrieben. Auswechselbarer außen gelegener Hauptstromölfilter. Ölfassungsvermögen des Ölsumpfes 3.5 Liter plus 0.6 Liter für den Filter.

Zündung: Unterdruckgeregelte, automatische Zündverstellung.

Kühlung: Druckkühlung mit Pumpe, Ventilator und Thermostat. Kühlerinhalt ca. 6 Liter.

Kupplung: Einscheibentrockenkupplung, Durchmesser 16 cm, hydraulisch betätigt.

Getriebe: Vier Gänge, im zweiten, dritten und vierten Gang synchronisiert. Übersetzungen: 1. Gang 3.628, 2. Gang 2.374, 3. Gang 1.412, 4. Gang 1.000. Rückwärtsgang: 4.664 : 1. Zentral montierter Fernschalthebel. Ölinhalt des Getriebes ca. 1.4 Liter.

Kardanwelle: Offen, mit Nadelrollenlager-Kreuzgelenken. Schiebekeile im Getriebe.

Hinterachse: Hypoid, dreiviertel-schwebend, Banjo-Typ. Übersetzungsverhältnis: 4.22:1 (9/38). Ölinhalt ca.1 Liter.

Gesamtübersetzungen: 1. Gang 15.31, 2. Gang 10.02, 3. Gang 596, 4. Gang 4.22. Rückwärtsgang 19.68.

Fahrgeschwindigkeiten bei 1000 U/min: 1.Gang 6.7 km/h, 2. Gang 10.3 km/h, 3. Gang 17.4 km/h, 4. Gang 24.6 km/h.

Lenkung: Zahnstangenlenkung, 2 ¹/₃-Drehungen von Einschlag zu Einschlag. Zweispeichenlenkrad, Durchmesser 41 cm. Wendekreis ca. 9.60 m.

Federung: Vorne unabhängig, mit Schwingarmhebeln, Spiralfedern und Stoßdämpfern. Rückwärts ¹/₄ elliptische Blattfedern mit Stoßdämpfern und Radiushebeln. Hydraulische Hebelstoßdämpfer.

Bremsen: Fußbremse, hydraulisch, auf alle vier Räder wirkend. Vorne zwei Bremsschuhe. Handbremse durch Kompensator auf Hinterräder wirkend; zentral montiert. Durchmesser 17.50 x 3.5 cm.

Though almost every fan of English sports cars at that time dreamed of a 100/6 or a 3000, these were too expensive for many young enthusiasts to afford and maintain. A way around the problem was offered in 1958 by the "Sprite", a highly originally designed little roadster with a frog's face and a one-liter four-cylinder motor under its hood, which could not work any wonders with its 46 HP but, thanks to its sportily Spartan nature, always gave the driver the feeling of going faster than he really was. Many drivers had their first experiences with sports cars in the narrow cockpit of a "Frogeye" Sprite.

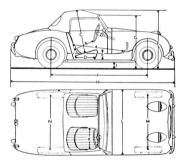

It was cramped in the Sprite's interior; large-size drivers had a hard time wedging themselves in ...

A Max.	A Min.	B Max	B Min.
1.10 m	1.00 m	0.43 m	0.36 m
C	**D**	**E**	**F**
0.88 m	0.48 m	0.20 m	1.26 m
G	**H**	**I**	**J**
1.12 m	3.49 m	2.03 m	0.13 m
K	**L**	**M**	**N**
0.43 m	1.35 m	1.16 m	1.14 m

Wendekreis	9.60 m
Ungefähres Gewicht (ohne Treibstoff)	597 kg

Turning circle ... 9.60 meters
Approx. weight (minus fuel) ... 597 kilograms

AUSTIN HEALEY

Sprite

OPEN FOR FAIR WEATHER . .

Whoever wanted a bit of comfort in rain or in winter weather could replace the drafty top with a hardtop available from the factory, as this rare special brochure shows.

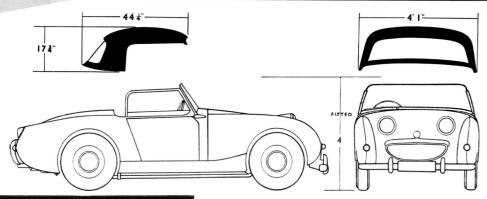

SPECIFICATION

This easily detachable unit is composed of a polyester resin-bonded fibreglass panel reinforced by an integral fibreglass framework.

Both interior and exterior panel faces are painted with a hard-wearing cellulose, while rubber sealing strips clipped to the panel edges form a perfect weatherproof joint when the Hard Top is fitted to the vehicle.

Excellent rearward vision is provided by a full-width double-curvature rear window, while sliding perspex side windows complete the all-weather protection.

Attaching the Hard Top to the car is quickly and easily effected by means of two flush-fitting toggle catches and two securing bolts and wing nuts, which fasten at the top corners of the windscreen and at the body sides respectively.

55

Though the whimsical appearance of the Sprite with the frog-eyes was a welcome joke for many, they spoiled the esthetic sensitivities of a great many interested parties, who backed off from making a purchase, especially in export markets.

Who can deny that this delightful addition to the marque of Austin Healey is aptly named? For although compact in proportion, the 'Sprite' nevertheless has a 'full-size' performance! The secret lies beneath the bonnet—power in plenty from the B.M.C. 'A' type engine fitted with twin S.U. carburetters and developing 42.5 b.h.p. at 5,000 r.p.m.!

THE EXCITING *New* AUSTIN HEALEY

AUSTIN HEALEY

Sprite

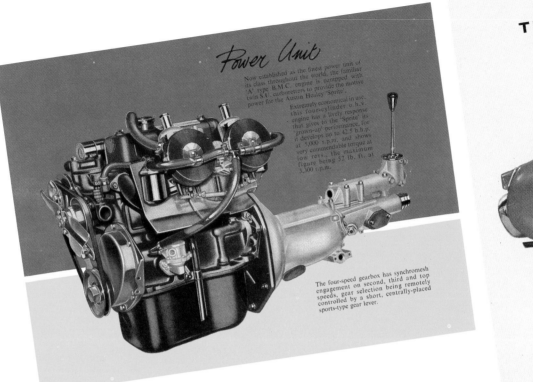

Power Unit

Now established as the finest power unit of its class throughout the world, the familiar 'A' type B.M.C. engine is equipped with twin S.U. carburetters to provide the motive power for the Austin Healey 'Sprite'.

Extremely economical in use, this four-cylinder o.h.v. engine has a lively response that gives to the 'Sprite' its 'grown-up' performance, for it develops up to 42.5 b.h.p. at 5,000 r.p.m. and shows very commendable torque at low revs, the maximum figure being 52 lb. ft. at 3,300 r.p.m.

The four-speed gearbox has synchromesh engagement on second, third and top speeds, gear selection being remotely controlled by a short, centrally-placed sports-type gear lever.

THE CAR T

The powerful little motor, the hard suspension setting and the exact shifting made sporty driving of the Sprite a pleasure, especially with the top down. Such "unnecessary extras" as door handles and locks and a trunk lid were dispensed with.

Brakes

Drive with confidence . . . for the powerful, four-wheel brakes are hydraulically operated by pendant pedal. There is also two-leading-shoe action on the front wheels, and for parking purposes the handbrake is mechanically connected to the rear wheels.

...FERS SO MUCH ····· FOR SO LITTLE ·····

There is much to interest the sports car enthusiast in the construction of this delightful newcomer to the world's sports car markets.

The designs of most of its major mechanical components have been proved in other B.M.C. models, so that to purchase a 'Sprite' is to have a ready-made, fully comprehensive, world-wide spares and service organisation!

Compact and 'clean', the body of the 'Sprite' is first completely immersed in a rust-inhibiting compound before receiving its finishing coats of high-lustre enamel, thus ensuring long, trouble-free life.

High quality P.V.C.-coated fabric is used entirely for the interior trim. Seats, casings and fascia panel are all covered with this hard-wearing material which, being washable, can be kept spotlessly clean.

The hood and sidescreens are also made from P.V.C.-coated fabric, forming a snug, weather-proof canopy which can be removed and stored in the rear compartment behind the seats when not in use.

Numerous items of optional equipment are available at small extra cost—such items as radio, heater, screen-washer and rev. counter can all be fitted to order. Robust overriders are fitted at the rear, and for extra protection at the front, a chromium plated bumper, complete with overriders, is fitted on all Export models, this being available at extra cost for the Home market.

COLOURS

The 'Sprite' is available in several combinations of exterior colours and interior trim, as set out in the panel below. In each case the road wheels are painted silver.

EXTERIOR COLOUR	INTERIOR TRIM COLOUR
Cherry red	Red with white piping and black or white hood.
Leaf green	Green with black or white hood.
Old English white	Red or black with white piping and black or white hood.
Iris blue	Blue with light blue piping and black or white hood.
Nevada beige	Red with white piping and black or white hood.

CAR PERFORMANCE ··········· ····· **SMALL CAR ECONOMY**

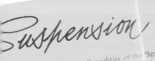

Suspension

The anti-roll qualities of the 'Sprite' are the result of its low centre of gravity and robust independent front suspension. Coil springs and wishbone connections are controlled by lever type hydraulic shock absorbers to give smooth, safe driving at all times.

Austin Healey Sprite Mark II

In 1961 the opponents of the "Frogeye" prevailed. The Sprite, now called Mark II, was given a new face with normal headlights built into the fenders. It was still a pretty car, but it had lost its special character. The rounded tail of the first version had likewise been reworked, making packing easier with a small trunk lid. Many mourned the end of the "Frogeye" Sprite; a bit of individuality in automobile construction had disappeared.

Naturally it was an advantage for everyone when the small luggage compartment could be reached through a normal lid instead of having to fold the seat forward and twist and turn to deposit one's belongings in a dark pit.

Gegen Aufpreis ist eine Sitzabdeckung, die jeweils zur Hälfte zurückgeschlagen werden kann, erhältlich. Sie ist so gearbeitet, daß sie rundum gut abdichtet und jedem Regenguß widersteht. Durch einen Stützbügel wird eine Wasseransammlung auf der Sitzabdeckung vermieden.

Obgleich für persönliches Kleingepäck viel Platz hinter den Sitzen zur Verfügung steht, können sperrige Dinge und das Reserverad im Kofferraum verschlossen aufbewahrt werden.

The Sprite Mark II, thanks to its new front-end design, looked almost like a "normal" car.

STIL UND CHARAKTER

Vom ersten Tage an hat sich der Austin Healy Sprite den Ruf eines kleinen Sportwagens mit großer Leistung geschaffen.

Der Austin Healy Sprite Typ II behält die Gediegenheit seines Vorgängers bei, ist aber nun — mit vermehrten PS und im neuen Gewand — mehr denn je unübertroffen an Qualität und Leistung in seiner Klasse.

Durchkonstruiert bis zum letzten, ist dieser jüngste Sprite ganz auf Fahrsicherheit gebaut, wie es nur bei neuzeitlichen Fertigungsmethoden möglich ist. Unabhängige Vorderrad-Einzelaufhängung, hydraulische Stoßdämpfer, Zahnstangenlenkung und ungewöhnlich niedriger Schwerpunkt sind Merkmale, die sich bei sorgfältiger Erprobung unter härtesten Bedingungen als verblüffend wirksam erwiesen haben, — Eigenschaften, die auch dem Austin Healy Sprite Typ II verliehen wurden, um das überraschende Fahrverhalten und die vorzügliche Straßenlage zu garantieren, die seinem Vorgänger schon die Herzen der sportlichen Fahrer in aller Welt zufliegen ließen.

Available at extra charge is a seat cover that can be folded back halfway. It is made so that it is watertight all the way around and withstands every hard rain. Water is prevented from gathering on the seat cover by a seat hoop.

Although there is much space for personal luggage behind the seats, valuable things and the spare wheel can be locked away in the luggage compartment.

STYLE AND CHARACTER

From the first day on, the Austin Healey Sprite has won the reputation of a small sports car with great performance.

The Austin Healey Sprite Type II maintains the quality of its forerunner, but is now—with increased HP and in a new dress—more than ever unexcelled in quality and performance in its class.

Well-built to the last detail, this young Sprite is built completely for driving safety, as is possible only with modern construction methods. Independent front suspension, hydraulic shock absorbers, rack-and-pinion steering and an unusually low center of gravity are features that have proved remarkably effective under careful testing.—Qualities that were also given to the Austin Healey Sprite Type II to guarantee the astonishing driving characteristics and outstanding roadholding that let its forerunner touch the hearts of sporting drivers all over the world.

Among the plentiful equipment is a coupe hardtop that turns the Sprite into a comfortable sport sedan. It is made of fiberglass and easy to remove. Thus every stretch of good weather can be enjoyed in an open car.

The interior decor is plentiful. All instruments and controls are easy to see and handily arranged near the driver.

Imitation leather was used for the upholstery. Seats, door coverings and dashboard are covered with this impervious material that can be kept spotlessly clean, since it is easily washable.

COMFORTABLE IN ALL WEATHER

The imitation leather folding top and mirror are kept in special pockets. The easily removed, aluminum-framed side windows are designed as sliding windows which can be opened easily to ventilate the car. These sliding windows are likewise usable with the coupe hardtop.

The door handles are located on the inside of the doors, which are likewise equipped with roomy open door pockets.

The two bucket seats are well upholstered. By an easily reached lever, the driver's and passenger's seats can be adjusted easily to fit individual needs.

The interior equipment of the Sprite is completed by a finely made, durable rubber mat to cover the front floor, while the luggage space behind the seats is covered in high-quality carpet material that matches the interior color.

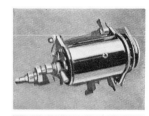

Zum reichhaltigen Zubehör gehört ein Coupé-Aufsatz, der den Sprite in eine komfortable Sportlimousine verwandelt. Er ist aus Fiberglas hergestellt und läßt sich leicht abnehmen. Somit kann jede Spanne günstigen Wetters im offenen Wagen genutzt werden.

Die Innenausstattung ist sehr umfangreich. Alle Instrumente und Bedienungsknöpfe sind übersichtlich und in bequemer Reichweite des Fahrers angeordnet.

Bei der Auskleidung wurde Kunstleder verwendet. Sitze, Tür-verkleidungen und Armaturenbrett sind mit diesem verschleißfesten Material bezogen, das makellos saubergehalten werden kann, da es leicht abwaschbar ist.

BEI JEDEM WETTER: WOHLBEHAGEN!

Kunstleder-Faltdach und Spiegel sind in Spezialtaschen verstaut. Die leicht abnehmbaren leichtmetallgefaßten Seitenfenster sind als Schiebefenster ausgebildet, die sich zur Belüftung des Wageninneren mühelos öffnen lassen. Diese Schiebefenster sind ebenfalls zum Coupé-Aufsatz verwendbar.

Die Türgriffe befinden sich an der Innenseite der Tür, die gleichzeitig mit geräumigen offenen Ablagefächern ausgestattet ist.

Die beiden Schalensitze sind gut gepolstert. Durch einen bequem zu erreichenden Hebel können sowohl Fahrer- als auch Beifahrersitz leicht verstellt und den individuellen Bedürfnissen angepaßt werden.

Die Innenausstattung des Sprite wird durch eine sauber gearbeitete, strapazierfähige Gummimatte, als Bodenbelag im Vorderteil, vervollständigt, während die Gepäckablage hinter den Sitzen mit hochwertigem Teppichmaterial ausgelegt ist, das farblich zum Innenraum paßt.

The motor of the Mark II brought three more horsepower, which had to suffice for a displacement of only 948 cc. Tested large-series technology made using the little sports car simple.

Scant sufficiency prevailed in the interior, snap-on window panels just barely kept out wind and rain.

1. Der Tourenzähler wird von der Lichtmaschine angetrieben.

2. Zwei SU Vergaser, Typ HS 2, sorgen für einwandfreie Beschleunigung.

3. Der Hauptstrom-Ölfilter, dessen Einsatz leicht auszu-wechseln ist, ist leicht zugänglich.

4. Die Zündung erfolgt durch eine Zünd-spule und automatische Zündverstellung.

1. The odometer is powered by the generator.
2. Two SU carburetors, Type HS 2, provide problem-free acceleration.
3. The mainstream oil filter, the element of which is easy to change, is easy to get at.
4. Ignition is done by a coil and an automatic distributor.
A robust frame-bottom construction and stable wheel suspension (independent front) made the Sprite a nimble car, very safe on curves.
5. The rear wheel suspension consists of quarter-elliptic leaf springs firmly anchored to the chassis frame and hydraulic shock absorbers.
6. To attain the greatest quiet while running and as low a center of gravity as possible, the rear axle was designed as a hypoid axle.
7. The rack-and-pinion steering allows direct contact with the road, which is so essential for this type of car. From block to block the 40-cm steering wheel needs only two and one-third turns.
8. The precise roadholding of the newest Sprite is attributable chiefly to the low center of gravity and the independent front suspension by wishbones and coil springs with double-acting hydraulic shock absorbers.

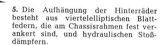

5. Die Aufhängung der Hinterräder besteht aus viertelelliptischen Blatt-federn, die am Chassisrahmen fest ver-ankert sind, und hydraulischen Stoß-dämpfern.

6. Zum Erreichen größter Laufruhe und eines möglichst niedrigen Schwerpunk-tes wurde die Hinterachse als Hypoid-Achse ausgebildet.

7. Die Zahnstangenlenkung vermittelt einen direkten Kontakt mit der Fahr-bahn, der für diese Art Wagen so we-sentlich ist. Von Anschlag zu Anschlag benötigt das 40 cm-Lenkrad nur $2^{1}/_{3}$ Umdrehungen.

8. Die genaue Spurhaltung des neu-esten Sprite ist weitgehendst auf die niedrige Schwerpunktlage und die Spur-haltung — Vorderrad-Einzelaufhängung an Trapezlenkern mit Schraubenfedern und doppelt wirkenden hydraulischen Stoßdämpfern — zurückzuführen.

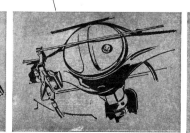

Austin Healey

SPRITE MK II

DATEN DES
AUSTIN HEALY SPRITE TYP II

MOTOR
Vierzylinder, obengesteuert, Bohrung 62,9 mm, Hub 76,2 mm, Hubraum 948 ccm, 46,5 PS bei 5 500 U/min; max. Drehmoment 7,20 m/kg bei 2 750 U/min.; Kompressionsverhältnis 9 : 1.
Schmierung: Die von der Nockenwelle angetriebene, konzentrische Zahnradölpumpe fördert das Öl zu allen beweglichen Teilen. Ölwannen-Inhalt (mit Filter): ca. 4 Liter.
Kühlung: Druckkühler mit Kreiselpumpe und Ventilator. Wasserzirkulations-Steuerung durch Thermostat. Kühlerinhalt: 5,7 Liter.
Treibstoffsystem: 2 Halbfallstrom - SU - Vergaser, Typ HS 2, durch Nockenwelle angetriebene Benzinpumpe. Tankinhalt: 27 Liter.
Zündsystem: Zündspule und -verteiler mit automatischem Fliehkraftregler und Vakuumverstellung.

CHASSIS
Kupplung: Hydraulische Einscheiben - Trockenkupplung 160 mm ⌀.
Getriebe: Viergang - Synchron - Getriebe; 2., 3. und 4. Gang synchronisiert. Ölinhalt: 1,33 Liter.
Getriebeübersetzung:
1. Gang = 3,2   2. Gang = 1,916
3. Gang = 1,357   4. Gang = 1,00
Rückwärtsgang = 4,114 : 1.
Direktschaltung mit zentral gelegenem Schalthebel.
Hinterachse: Hypoid verzahnt 4,22 : 1. Ölinhalt: 1 Liter.
Übersetzungsverhältnisse: 1. Gang 13,5; 2. Gang 8,08;
3. Gang 5,72; 4. Gang 4,22; Rückwärtsgang 17,38 : 1.
Direktschaltung mit zentral gelegenem Schalthebel.
Gelenkwelle: Nadelgelagert.

Lenkung: Zahnstangen-Lenkung, Zweispeichen-Lenkrad, ⌀ 41 cm.
Aufhängung: vorn: Einzelradaufhängung mit Schraubenfedern und Tragarmen.
hinten: Viertelelliptische Blattfedern.
Bremsen: vorn und hinten: Hydraulische Stoßdämpfer. Durch hängendes Bremspedal betätigte, hydraulische Bremsen. Die mechanische Handbremse mit zentral gelegenem Handbremshebel wirkt auf die Hinterräder; Trommeldurchmesser 178 mm, Bremsbackenbreite 31,8 mm.
Räder und Bereifung: Stahlpreßräder mit Ventilationslöchern und 4 Befestigungsbolzen; 5,20 × 13 schlauchlose Reifen.

ELEKTRISCHE AUSRÜSTUNG
12 Volt-Anlage, Batterie 38/10 amp/h Leistung, Fußabblendschalter, Seitenlampen kombiniert mit bernsteinfarbenen Frontblinkern, doppelte Stop-Schlußlampen mit roten Reflektoren und roten Blinkern, Warnlampen mit Armaturenbrett zur Kontrolle von Winker- und Lichtmaschinenfunktion sowie Fernlicht. Doppelte Scheibenwischer, Starkton-Horn, kombiniertes Sicherheitslenk-, steck- und Zündschloß.

INSTRUMENTE
Geschwindigkeitsmesser mit separatem Tages-Kilometerzähler, Benzinuhr, Fernthermometer und Öldruckanzeiger kombiniert.

KAROSSERIE
Zweitüriger Zweisitzer mit selbsttragender Stahlkarosserie. Die Motorhaube ist von vorn zu öffnen und wird vom Wageninneren gesichert. Die Kofferraumklappe ist verschließbar. Gebogene Windschutzscheibe aus Sicherheitsglas im polierten Aluminiumrahmen, abnehmbare Seitenteile; Innenverkleidung einschließlich Armaturenbrett mit Kunstleder ausgestattet, hinter den Sitzen eingepaßtes Teppichmaterial, Fahrer- und Beifahrersitz verstellbar. Beide Sitze haben Schaumgummikissen und Rükkenlehnen aus gummiertem Polsterhaar. Eingebaute Befestigungsvorrichtung für Sicherheitsgurte (Sicherheitsgurte sind ein erprobtes Zubehör, das über den B.M.C.-Service Ltd. bezogen werden kann). Beide Wagentüren haben Innenschloß und offenes Ablegefach. Das Fahrgastraum mit Gummimatten ausgelegt. Reserverad ist horizontal im Kofferraum montiert. Das abnehmbare Kunstlederverdeck kann mit seinen Spriegeln und Seitenteilen in den dafür vorgesehenen Spezialtaschen im Kofferraum verstaut werden. Hinten schützen verchromte Stoßstangenhörner die Karosserie, Beifahrer-Haltegriff, Innenspiegel.

EXTRA - ZUBEHÖR
Radio; Sitzabdeckung mit Stützbügel; verschließbarer Tankdeckel; Zigarrenanzünder; Rad-Zierkappen; abnehmbarer Coupé-Aufsatz; Weißwandreifen; verstärkte Spezialbereifung; Zweiklanghorn; Gepäckständer; Kokosmatten (Natur).

Mehr über den Sprite . . . . . sagt Ihnen gern jeder Besitzer

AUSTIN MOTOR EXPORT CORPORATION LIMITED
LONGBRIDGE · BIRMINGHAM · ENGLAND

THE AUSTIN MOTOR COMPANY LIMITED
BIRMINGHAM
LONGBRIDGE

Printed in England

Austin Healey Sprite Mk. II
DATA ON THE AUSTIN HEALEY S

MOTOR
Four-cylinder, overhead-camshaft, bore 62.9 mm, stroke 76.2 displacement 948 cc, 46.5 HP at 5500 rpm, maximum torque m/kg at 2750 rpm, compression ratio 9:1.
Lubrication: The concentric geared oil pump driven by the cams drives the iol to all moving parts. Oilpan capacity (with f approximately 4 liters.
Cooling: Pressure cooling with circulating pump and radiator. W circulation controlled by thermostat. Radiator capacity: 5.7 liter Fuel system: 2 semi-downdraft SU carburetors, Type HS 2, fuel p driven by the camshaft. Tank capacity: 27 liters.
Ignition system: Coil and distributor with automatic voltage regu and vacuum adjustment.

CHASSIS
Clutch: Hydraulic single-plate dry clutch, 160 mm diameter.
Gears: Synchronized four-speed gearbox, 2nd, 3rd and 4th synchronized. Oil capacity: 1.33 liter. Gear ratios: 1st gear ' 3.2 gear ' 1.916, 3rd gear ' 1.357, 4th gear ' 1.00, reverse ' 4.114:1. E shifting by centrally mounted shift lever.
Rear axle: Hypoid geared, 4.22:1, oil capacity: 1 liter. Transmi ratios: 1st gear 13.5, 2nd gear 8.08, 3rd gear 5.72, 4th gear 4.22, re 17.38:1. Direct shifting by centrally mounted shift lever. Drives needle bearings.
Steering: Rack-and-pinion steering, two-spoke steering w diameter 41 cm.
Suspension: Front: Independent suspension with coil springs wishbones. Rear: Quarter-elliptic leaf springs. Front and hydraulic shock absorbers.
Brakes: Operated by hanging brake pedal, hydraulic brakes. mechanical hand brake with centrally located lever works on the wheels; drum diameter 178 mm, brake-shoe width 31.8 mm.
Wheels and tires: Pressed steel wheels with ventilation holes and attaching lugs; 5.20 x 13 tubeless tires.

ELECTRICAL EQUIPMENT
12-volt system, battery 38/10 amp/h power, foot dimmer switch lamps combined with amber front directional lights, double b taillights with red reflectors and directional lights; indicator lig dashboard for directionals and generator as well as high beams. windshield wipers, strong-tone horn, combined safety steering and ignition lock.

INSTRUMENTS
Speedometer with separate daily odometer, fuel gauge, thermor and oil pressure gauge combined.

BODYWORK
Two-door two-seater with self-bearing steel body. The motor opens from the front and is unlatched from inside the car. The t lid locks. Bowed windshield of safety glass in polished alum. frame, removable side pieces; interior including dashboard co with imitation leather, matching carpet meterial behind the adjustable driver's and passenger's seats. Both seats have foam r padding and backs of rubberized felt. Built-in attachment poin seat belts (seat belts are a tested accessory that can be ordered B.M.C. Service Ltd.)
Interior includes rubber mats. Both car doors have inside lock open pockets. The spare wheel is located horizontally in the t The removable imitation leather top can, with its hoops and pieces, be stowed in the special pockets provided for it in the lu space. At the rear, chromed bumper overriders protect the l Passenger handhold, inside mirror. EXTRA EQUIPMENT
Radio; seat cover with support hoop; locking filler cap; cig lighter; hubcaps; removable coupe roof; whitewall tires; strength special tires; two-tone horn; luggage rack; (natural) coconut ma
More about the Sprite . . . any owner will tell you.

Even a trunk-lid lock was standard equipment now, but the side doors could still be locked only from inside.

At night the headlights, now conventionally located, lit up the street, while the sight conditions with the top up could not exactly be described as ideal.

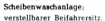

Um den Weltmarktansprüchen zu genügen, gehört zur Standardausführung des Austin Healy Sprite Typ II „Export" folgende Ausrüstung:

Vordere und hintere Stoßstange mit Stoßstangenhörnern; Tourenzähler; Scheibenwaschanlage; verstellbarer Beifahrersitz.

EXPORT AUSSTATTUNG

Ohne Aufpreis wird das Exportmodell in nachstehenden Variationen geliefert:

Rechts- oder Linkslenkung;
Meilen- oder Kilometerzähler;
Scheinwerfer und Blinker entsprechend den Vorschriften des jeweiligen Einfuhrlandes.

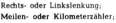

Sonder-Zubehör gegen Aufpreis:
Radio; Sitzabdeckung mit Stützbügel; Windschutzscheibe aus Verbundglas; verschließbarer Tankdeckel; Zigarrenanzünder; abnehmbarer Coupé-Aufsatz; Weißrandreifen; sechsfach verstärkte Bereifung für höchste Ansprüche; Zweiklanghorn; Gepäckständer.

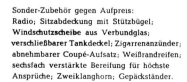

Die in diesem Prospekt enthaltenen Angaben sind zur Zeit der Publikation richtig; Änderungen können aber ohne vorherige Mitteilung vorgenommen werden.

EXPORT VERSION

To satisfy world-market demands, the standard equipment of the Austin Healey Sprite Type II "Export" includes the following equipment:
Front and rear bumpers with overriders, tachometer, windshield washer system, adjustable passenger seat.
At no extra charge, the Export model is available in the following versions:
Right or left-hand drive;
Speedometer in miles or kilometers;
Headlights and directionals corresponding to the regulations of the import country.
Special equipment at extra charge:
Radio; seat cover with support hoop; laminated glass windshield; locking filler cap; cigarette lighter; removable coupe hardtop; whitewall tires; six-ply reinforced tires to meet highest demands; two-tone horn; luggage rack.
The information in this brochure is correct at the time of publication, but changes can be made without notification in advance.

The standard export version of the Mark II with adjustable passenger seat and windshield washer system was almost luxurious.

The Victor in International Races

Much about the Austin Healey Sprite Type II will interest the sports-car fan. The feeling of driving it gives the sensation of the performance of big sports cars and the impression of extraordinary agility of small ones, in whose class the Sprite is unchallenged. At the same time, the characteristic of its outstanding economy is all the more noteworthy. Its performance on all the world's roads is legendary. From the smallest loacl club meet to the great international rally, it goes without saying that the Sprite ranks among those that reach the finish line victorious.

The secret of this astonishing success is under the motor hood. The temperament and power of the proven B.M.C. A-Type motor with two carburetors, now brought to hitherto unheard-of performance without any loss of long life and reliability. Plus direct shifting with the centrally located shift lever. All of this means more liveliness, more temperament and increasing driving enjoyment with every kilometer. In agreement with the British Motor Corporation's standardization efforts, the main components are identical to those of other B.M.C. vehicles; thus when one buys a Sprite one finds a ready, all-inclusive worldwide spare-part and service network available!

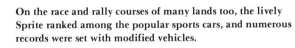

Den Sportwagenfreund interessiert vieles am Austin Healy Sprite Typ II. Das Fahrgefühl vermittelt das Empfinden der Leistung großer Sportwagen und den Eindruck außerordentlicher Wendigkeit der kleinen, in deren Bereich der Sprite unbestritten führt. Umso hervorstechender ist gleichzeitig das Merkmal seiner ausgesprochenen Wirtschaftlichkeit. . .

Seine Leistungen auf allen Straßen der Welt sind sagenhaft. Vom kleinsten örtlichen Klubkampf bis zur größten internationalen Rallye gilt es als selbstverständlich, daß der Sprite unter denen rangiert, die erfolgreich ins Ziel kommen.

Das Geheimnis seiner erstaunlichen Erfolge liegt unter der Motorhaube: Temperament und Kraft durch den bewährten B.M.C. „A"-Typ Motor mit zwei Vergasern, der jetzt auf bisher unerreichte Leistung gebracht wurde ohne an Lebensdauer und Zuverlässigkeit zu verlieren. Dazu die Direktschaltung mit zentral gelegenem Schalthebel. Dies alles bedeutet mehr Spritzigkeit, mehr Temperament und mit jedem Kilometer zunehmendes Fahrvergnügen.

In Übereinstimmung mit den Normungsbestrebungen der British Motor Corporation sind die hauptsächlichen Bestandteile mit denen der anderen B.M.C.-Fahrzeuge identisch; so findet man beim Kauf eines Sprite einen einsatzbereiten, alles umfassenden, weltweiten Ersatzteil- und Kundendienst vor!

On the race and rally courses of many lands too, the lively Sprite ranked among the popular sports cars, and numerous records were set with modified vehicles.

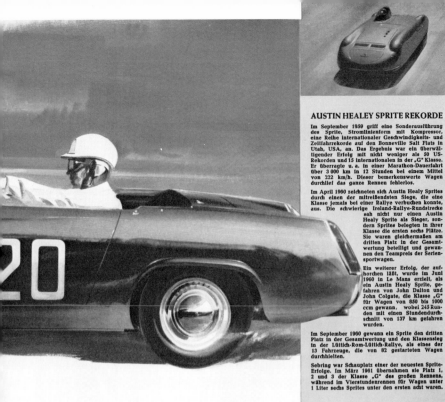

AUSTIN HEALEY SPRITE REKORDE

Im September 1959 griff eine Sonderausführung des Sprite, Stromlinienform mit Kompressor, eine Reihe internationaler Geschwindigkeits- und Zeitfahrrekorde auf den Bonneville Salt Flats in Utah, USA, an. Das Ergebnis war ein überwältigender Erfolg mit nicht weniger als 50 US-Rekorden und 15 internationalen in der „G" Klasse. Er überragte u. a. in einer Marathon-Dauerfahrt über 3 000 km in 12 Stunden bei einem Mittel von 222 km/h. Dieser bemerkenswerte Wagen durchlief das ganze Rennen fehlerlos.

Im April 1960 zeichneten sich Austin Healy Sprites durch einen der mitreißendsten Siege, die eine Klasse jemals bei einer Rallye verbuchen konnte, aus. Die schwierige Ireland-Rallye-Rundstrecke sah nicht nur einen Austin Healy Sprite als Sieger, sondern Sprites belegten in ihrer Klasse die ersten sechs Plätze. Sie waren gleichermaßen am dritten Platz in der Gesamtwertung beteiligt und gewannen den Teampreis der Serien-sportwagen.

Ein weiterer Erfolg, der aufhorchen ließt, wurde im Juni 1960 in Le Mans erzielt, als ein Austin Healy Sprite, gefahren von John Dalton und John Colgate, die Klasse „G" für Wagen von 850 bis 1000 ccm gewann, wobei 245 Runden mit einen Stundendurchschnitt von 137 km gefahren wurden.

Im September 1960 gewann ein Sprite den dritten Platz in der Gesamtwertung und den Klassensieg in der Lüttich-Rom-Lüttich-Rallye, als eines der 13 Fahrzeuge, die von 82 gestarteten Wagen durchhielten.

Sebring war Schauplatz einer der neuesten Sprite-Erfolge. Im März 1961 übernahmen sie Platz 1, 2 und 3 der Klasse „G" des großen Rennens, während im Vierstundenrennen für Wagen unter 1 Liter sechs Sprites unter den ersten acht waren.

AUSTIN HEALEY SPRITE RECORDS

In September of 1959 a special version of the Sprite, with streamlined body and supercharger, set a number of international speed records on the Bonneville Salt Flats in Utah, USA. The result was a resounding success, with no fewer than 50 US and 15 international records in Class G. In a marathon endurance run, it covered, among others, over 3000 km in 12 hours at a speed of 222 kph. This remarkable car made the entire run problem-free.

In April of 1960 Austin Healey Sprites achieved one of the most outstanding victories that a class ever scored in a rally. The challenging Ireland Rally course saw not only an Austin Healey Sprite as the victor, but Sprites won the first six places in their class. They likewise won third place in the general classification and won the team prize for production sports cars.

Another success worth noting was won at Le Mans in July of 1960 when an Austin Healey Sprite driven by John Dalton and John Colgate won Class G for cars from 850 to 1000 cc, covering 245 laps at an average speed of 137 kph.

In September of 1960 a Sprite won third place in the general classification and a class victory in the Liege-Rome-Liege Rally, as one of the 13 cars to finish out of 82 starters.

Sebring was the showplace of one of the Sprite's newest successes. In March of 1961 they took 1st, 2nd and 3rd places in Class G of the great race, while in a four-hour race for cars under one liter six Sprites finished in the first eight.

Below: A 1962 sales brochure referred to the new 1100-cc motor with approximately 55 horsepower, which gave a top speed of over 140 kph.

...and now even faster!

The Austin Healey Sprite Mark II—already leading its class in performance, comfort and safety, offers as of now even more value for your money. Please compare the following improvements with the corresponding brochure listings.

More powerful motor: With an increased bore (to 64.58 mm) and stroke (to 83.72 mm), the new SPRITE now has a displacement of 1083 cc. The crankshaft was strengthened and a high-performance sport camshaft was used. Piston rods and oil ducts in the crankcase were changed. With larger inlet ports in the cylinder head, the renowned BMC A-series motor now produces 55 HP at 5750 rpm.

Easier shifting: A strengthened clutch with 18.41-cm diameter transmits the higher engine power. With free ring synchronization in 2nd, 3rd and 4th gears, the gears can be shifted easily and quickly. The needle bearings of the driveshaft were enlarged. The gearbox is also ribbed now; this makes it more stable, more quiet and better cooled.

Disc brakes: Along with the greater power, naturally particular attention was devoted to improved safety. The front wheels have disc brakes of 21-cm diameter. The main brake cylinder was equipped with a modified filler to avoid overfilling.

Roadholding and handling are even better: The handling of the Sprite, already renowned in sporting circles, was improved by standard equipping with tubeless Gold Seal C 41 tires.

Improved interior equipment: The upper edges of the seat area were equipped with an upholstered ridge. Now both seats are adjustable. The whole floor surface is covered with durable carpeting. The dashboard was redesigned and an electric tachometer is now included in the standard equipment.

New hardtop: The form of the two-piece sliding side windows was changed to suit the new hardtop design. This new hardtop is available at extra charge.

New colors: From now on, the wishes of the young sporting driver are fulfilled amd the dark BRITISH RACING GREEN is included in the popular and familiar array of colors.

... ünd nün noch schneller!

Der Austin Healey Sprite Mk II - bisher schon in Leistung, Komfort und Sicherheit in seiner Klasse führend, bietet ab sofort noch mehr Gegenwert für Ihr gutes Geld. Vergleichen Sie bitte die nachfolgenden Verbesserungen mit den entsprechenden Prospektangaben.

Stärkerer Motor Durch die Vergrößerung von Bohrung (auf 64,58 mm) und Hub (auf 83,72 mm) hat der neue SPRITE nunmehr einen Hubraum von 1083 ccm. Die Kurbelwelle wurde verstärkt und eine Hochleistungs-Sport-Nockenwelle verwendet. Kolben und Ölzuleitungen im Kurbelwellengehäuse wurden verändert. Mit größeren Einlaßöffnungen im Zylinderkopf leistet der bekannte BMC A-Serienmotor jetzt 55 PS bei 5750 U/min.

Leichteres Schalten Eine verstärkte Kupplung mit 18,41 cm Durchmesser trägt der höheren Motorleistung Rechnung. Durch freitragende Ring-Synchronisation im 2., 3. und 4. Gang läßt sich das Getriebe leicht und schnell schalten. Die Nadellager der Hauptwelle wurden vergrößert. Das Getriebegehäuse ist nun außen verrippt; dadurch ist es stabiler, geräuschmildernder und kühlungsfördernd.

Scheibenbremsen Entsprechend der größeren Leistung wurde selbstverständlich auch besonderer Wert auf erhöhte Sicherheit gelegt. An den Vorderrädern befinden sich Scheibenbremsen von 21 cm Durchmesser. Der Hauptbremszylinder wurde mit einer geänderten Einfüllöffnung versehen, die ein Überfüllen verhindert.

Straßenlage und Bodenhaftung noch besser Das in Sportkreisen schon immer gerühmte Fahrverhalten des Sprite wurde nunmehr durch serienmäßige Ausrüstung mit schlauchlosen Gold Seal C 41 Reifen noch verbessert.

Verbesserte Innenausstattung Die Oberkanten des Sitzraumes sind nun rundum mit einem Posterwulst versehen. Jetzt sind beide Sitze verstellbar. Die gesamte Bodenfläche ist mit dauerhaftem Teppich ausgelegt. Das Armaturenbrett wurde neu gestaltet und ein elektrischer Drehzahlmesser gehört jetzt zur serienmäßigen Ausstattung.

Neues Hardtop Die Form der zweiteiligen, seitlichen Schiebefenster wurde geändert und dem neu gestalteten Hardtop angepaßt. Dieses neue Hardtop ist gegen Aufpreis erhältlich.

Neue Farben Nunmehr wurde auch der Wunsch der jungen Sportfahrer erfüllt und das dunkle BRITISH RACING GREEN zur Vervollständigung in die beliebte und bekannte Farbskala aufgenommen.

The low costs and excellent racing suitability of the Austin Healey Sprite inspired a number of firms, especially in Britain, to specialize in tuning these cars. From a supercharger to a special body, practically every wish for higher performance or other improvement could be fulfilled. A fullness of advertising material made the choice a hard one.

AUSTIN HEALEY SEBRING SPRITE

This fabulous high performance version of the Austin Healey Sprite was first introduced in 1959 as a small, fast grand touring car with exceptional road holding and braking, to effectively cope with modern traffic conditions and high speed Motorway travel. Since that time, many owners have regularly used their Sebring Sprites in all forms of competition with outstanding results, and indeed, the name itself is derived from three successive class victories in the International Sebring G.T. and Sports Car races held annually in Florida.

Whilst the majority of Sebring Sprites are used as exhilarating personal transport, the factory is naturally aware that many are also in constant use for race and rally, and with this competitive requirement in mind, the cars have been fully recognised by the F.I.A. as standard production Grand Touring cars.

Sebring modifications can be carried out to customer's own cars – or to new vehicles and in either case carry a twelve month warranty. The comprehensive specification, with choice of six stages of engine tune ranging from 55 to 87 b.h.p. can be varied to suit the individual tastes and requirements of the owner and this includes such items as interior trim, colour, instrumentation, radio, lighting, final drive ratios and safety belts.

Liege-Rome-Liege Rally 1960

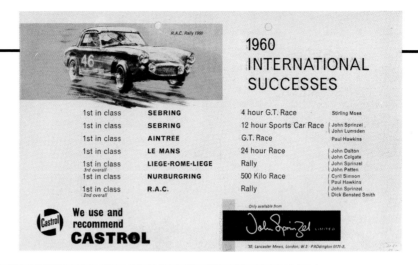

1960 INTERNATIONAL SUCCESSES

R.A.C. Rally 1960

1st in class	**SEBRING**	4 hour G.T. Race	Stirling Moss	
1st in class	**SEBRING**	12 hour Sports Car Race	John Sprinzel / John Lumsden	
1st in class	**AINTREE**	G.T. Race	Paul Hawkins	
1st in class	**LE MANS**	24 hour Race	John Dalton / John Colgate	
1st in class 3rd overall	**LIEGE-ROME-LIEGE**	Rally	John Sprinzel / John Patten	
1st in class	**NURBURGRING**	500 Kilo Race	Cyril Simson / Paul Hawkins	
1st in class 2nd overall	**R.A.C.**	Rally	John Sprinzel / Dick Bensted Smith	

We use and recommend **CASTROL**

Only available from

John Sprinzel LIMITED

32, Lancaster Mews, London, W.2. PADdington 0171-2.

John Sprinzel Ltd. of London also offered a number of modifications to prepare the Sprite for the demands of racing. This firm's successful racing versions attained up to 87 HP. The rally champion Sprinzel even put out his own brochures.

Clutch: Single dry plate 6¼″ diameter. Hydraulic operation, six spring for road use, nine spring for competition.

Final drive ratios: and gear ratios: various alternatives are available to suit most requirements.

Suspension: Front independent, with wishbones, coil springs, anti-roll bar and radius arms rear quarter elliptic leaf springs; lever type hydraulic heavy duty shock absorbers.

Steering: Rack and pinion – 2¼ turns of 15″ diameter wood rimmed steering wheel lock to lock. Turning circle approx. 31′ 6″.

Brakes: 8¼″ Front girling disc brakes, rear 8″ drums, fully hydraulic.

Road Wheels: balanced 60 spoke Dunlop racing wheels, with centre knock-on chrome hubs. 5.20 x 13″ tyres with tubes. Dunlop Duraband RB1 or Dunlop Racing R5 tyres.

Fuel System: AC type "Y" mechanical pump on "Road", "Supercharged" and "Sport" models. S.U. electric pump on "Competition", "Race" and "Bonneville" models. Tank capacity 6 gallons, competition 11 gallons.

Lubrication: Full pressure feed wet sump system, with full flow external oil filter and full flow oil cooler.

Ignition System: Coil and distributor. Spark plugs appropriate to degree of engine tune.

Instruments: Speedometer with trip reading, petrol gauge, combined water temperature and oil pressure gauge, ignition, flasher and high beam indicators, revolution counter. Ammeter, Halda Speedpilot, etc., optional.

Bodywork: Two-door, two seater steel mono-construction. Optional aluminium bodywork. Front-hinged fibreglass bonnet. Detachable fibreglass hardtop, or `fixed head coupe in aluminium with curved laminated windscreen. Interior trim in rubber with PVC covered panels, or full de-luxe carpeting and sound proofing. Fibreglass competition seats available.

Weight: The road version weighs approximately 13 cwt (without fuel) competition versions can be brought down to 11¼ cwt.
A complete range of lighting, heaters, radios, and rally equipment can be supplied on the Sebring Sprite.

SEBRING ROAD In-line 4 cylinder OHV watercooled, three bearing counter-balanced crankshaft. Bore 2.478″. Stroke 3″. Cubic capacity 948 c.c. Fitted with high compression solid-skirt pistons, sports camshaft and matching distributor, three branch exhaust system and silencer, 7,000 r.p.m. valve springs. Modified inlet ports and combustion chambers 9.0 to 1 compression ratio, approximately 55 b.h.p.

SEBRING SUPERCHARGED As above, but with low compression pistons, touring camshaft, Shorrock supercharger, vane type, copper/asbestos/steel cylinder head gasket, low compression cylinder head, 7,000 r.p.m. valve springs, approximately 68 b.h.p.

SEBRING SPORTS A 'Road' version, but with enlarged inlet valves polished and contoured combustion chambers, twin 1¼″ SU carburetters on Healey speed manifolds with balance pipe and heat shield. 9.3 to 1 compression ratio, approximately 62 b.h.p.

SEBRING COMPETITION As 'Sports' version but bored out to 2.538″ giving 995 c.c. Fitted with special camshaft bearings, balanced and lightened flywheel, crankshaft, nine spring competition clutch, competition cylinder head gasket, SU electric pump. 10.0 to 1 compression ratio. Approximately 70 b.h.p.

SEBRING RACE Intended only for use on the track, in addition to the 'Competition' specification, this version has a special material racing crankshaft, the engine is balanced throughout, and the cylinder head is modified to full formula 'Junior' tune. Compression ratio up to 11.0 to 1 from 75 to 80 b.h.p.

BONNEVILLE SUPERCHARGED Also intended solely for racing, this version uses a Shorrocks supercharger in place of the twin SU's and a specially modified cylinder head. Otherwise as the 'Race' tune. Approximately 87 b.h.p.

The most powerful street version by John Sprinzel, who had won the class victory at Sebring in 1960, produced 70 HP with a compression ratio of 10:1.

STYLE AND PERFORMANCE ... WITH SOFT OR HARD TOP

Here is a brochure that looks very different from the usual ones, its message concentrated in the simple form of the car.

Arrangement of rear bumper and overriders, which, together with front bumper and overriders, is standard equipment on all export vehicles.

Austin Healey

SPRITE MK II

specification

| De-Luxe Model

The Mark II was built until 1964. It stood out in functionality and simplicity of construction and offered its owners a high degree of driving pleasure.

LEADING DIMENSIONS

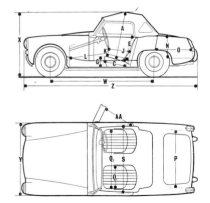

AA 2ft. 2in. (0.66 m.)	**A** 2ft. 10½in. (0.86 m.)	**C** 1ft. 7in. (0.48 m.)	**E** 1ft. 7in. (0.48 m.)
G 8½in. (0.22 m.)	**J** (min.) 1ft. 1½in. (0.35 m.)	**J** (max.) 1ft. 5½in. (0.44 m.)	**K** 5in. (0.13 m.)
L (min.) 3ft. 5in. (1.04 m.)	**L** (max.) 3ft. 8½in. (1.13 m.)	**N** 1ft. 3½in. (0.39 m.)	**O** 2ft. 3½in. (0.70 m.)
P 3ft. 6in. (1.07 m.)	**Q₁** 1ft. 5in. (0.43 m.)	**Q₂** 3ft. 8½in. (1.12 m.)	**S** 4ft. 0½in. (1.23 m.)
W 6ft. 8in. (2.03 m.)	**X** (Hood raised) 4ft. 1½in. (1.26 m.)	**X** (Hood lowered) 3ft. 7in. (1.09 m.)	**Y** 4ft. 5in. (1.35 m.)
Z 11ft. 0½in. (3.37 m.)	**Z** (With front & rear bumpers & overriders) 11ft. 5⅞ in (3.50 m.)	**Track** (Front) 3ft. 9½in. (1.16 m.)	**Track** (Rear) 3ft. 8½in. (1.14 m.)
Turning Circle 32ft. (9.75 m.)	**Approx. Weight** 11 cwt. 3 qr. (597 kg.)		

THE AUSTIN MOTOR COMPANY LIMITED
LONGBRIDGE - - - - - - - - - - - BIRMINGHAM
AUSTIN MOTOR EXPORT CORPORATION LIMITED
LONGBRIDGE - - - - - BIRMINGHAM - - - - - ENGLAND

The bucket seats and cockpit ★
are designed for maximum efficiency
and minimum fatigue over long-
distance driving. Seats are individually
adjustable and contoured for greater
comfort, upholstered in a variety
of durable trim colours.

The floor and transmission tunnel ★
are covered in high-quality thick
carpet. In fact, everything inside the
M.G. Midget (Mk. II) is tailored
for your comfort and safety.
A thick safety padded roll tops the
fascia. Gear lever and hand brake are
within easy reach.

Look into the Mark II **MG** Midget

The Twin Brother: MG Midget

Since July of 1961 there was an almost identical brother of the Sprite within the BMC Group, with the name of Midget and the MG emblem on its trunk lid. A lateral chrome strip, different radiator grille and more elegant interior constituted its difference from the Sprite. MG wanted to fill out its sports-car program at the lower end by this somewhat unusual means.

★ **The semi-elliptic rear suspension** has been designed primarily for even higher cornering ability with minimum roll. They replace the formerly used quarter elliptics; thereby steering and lateral stability are greatly improved, permitting faster cornering, whilst at the same time considerably lessening road shocks.

Take another look

at the Mk II specification

★ Space—at a premium in most cars—is available to a considerable degree in the Mark II Midget—there is room behind the seats for luggage, or for carrying a third person for short distances. There is more room still in the boot—plenty of lockable luggage space for your touring kit. Couple it with M.G. performance, instant weather protection . . .

. . . which is assured by the new winding windows and a hood that is simple to erect. The durable and completely waterproof hood blends beautifully with the smooth lines of the car and has a large rear window area for continued good visibility with the car closed.

> Neue Aufhängung!
> Stärker und ruhiger!
> Luxuriöse Ausstattung des Cockpits!

SPRITE MK III
SPORT CONVERTIBLE

DER NEUE *Austin Healey*

New suspension!
Stronger and quieter!
Luxurious cockpit furnishing!
The new Austin Healey Sprite Mk. II sport convertible

As with the big Austin Healey, so too did the development of the Sprite move steadily away from the essential, Spartan sporting vehicle toward the well-appointed and comparatively comfortable small sports car. Many may have regretted this development, but on the other hand it is understandable that a manufacturer has to be guided by customers' wishes, especially those from a major market in a foreign land, where a touch of comfort is more important than the expression of sportiness in the rugged old English tradition. The Sprite Mark III, introduced in 1964, also met these demands quite clearly.

Bewährtes BMC-Zubehör:

Jeder Austin-Händler wird Sie gern beim Kauf dieses Zubehörs beraten. Folgendes Zubehör wird von der BMC speziell für Ihren Sprite empfohlen:

1. Außenspiegel
2. Montagelampe
3. Sitzkissen, hinten
4. Feuerlöscher
5. Plakettenstange
6. Gepäckträger
7. Ausbesserungslack
8. Werkzeug
9. Sicherheitsgurte
10. Gummimatten
11. Schonbezüge

A popular item of Sprite equipment was the sportily chic seat cover (tonneau cover) which could be opened for the driver's seat alone.

Die Sitzabdeckung, die jeweils zur Hälfte zurückgeschlagen werden kann, ist so gearbeitet, daß sie rundum gut abdichtet und jedem Regenguß widersteht. Durch einen Stützbügel wird eine Wasseransammlung auf der Sitzabdeckung vermieden.

Obgleich für persönliches Kleingepäck viel Platz hinter den Sitzen zur Verfügung steht, können sperrige Dinge und das Reserverad im Kofferraum verschlossen aufbewahrt werden.

Proven BMC Accessories:
Every Austin dealer will gladly advise you as to the purchase of these accessories. The following accessories are especially recommended for your Sprite by BMC:
1. Outside mirror
2. Plug-in lamp
3. Rear seat cushion
4. Fire extinguisher
5. Signpost
6. Luggage rack
7. Touch-up paint
8. Tools
9. Seat belt
10. Rubber mats
11. Protective covers
The seat cover, which can be opened halfway from either side, is made so that it is watertight all around and withstands any heavy rain. A support hoop prevents water from collecting on the seat cover. Although there is plenty of room for personal luggage behind the seats, valuable things and the spare wheel can be locked away in the trunk.

Export-Ausstattung

Um den Weltmarktansprüchen zu genügen, gehört zur Standardausführung des Austin-Healey Sprite MK III „Export" folgende Ausrüstung:

Vordere und hintere Stoßstange mit Stoßstangenhörnern; elektrischer Tourenzähler, Scheibenwaschanlage, Frischluftheizung, verstellbare Sitze, Sitzabdeckung, Lenkschloß. Ohne Aufpreis wird das Exportmodell in nachstehenden Variationen geliefert.

Rechts- oder Linkslenkung; Meilen- oder Kilometerzähler; Scheinwerfer und Blinker entsprechend den Vorschriften des jeweiligen Landes.

Sonder-Zubehör gegen Aufpreis:

Radio, Windschutzscheibe aus Verbundglas, verschließbarer Tankdeckel. Zigarrenanzünder, Zweiklanghorn, Sitzkissen hinten, Gepäckständer, Cocosmatten, Holzlenkrad, Kühlerjalousie, Speichenräder, Querstabilisator, Lichthupe.

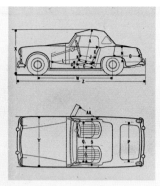

ABMESSUNGEN

AA	J (min)	C	E
0,66 m	0,35 m	0,48 m	0,48 m
G	L (max)	J (max)	K
0,22 m	1,13 m	0,44 m	0,13 m
L (min)	Q1	N	O
1,04 m	0,43 m	0,39 m	0,70 m
P		Q2	S
1,07 m	X	1,12 m	1,23 m
W	Verdeck ob.	X	Y
2,03 m	1,26 m	Verdeck unt. 1,09 m	1,35 m
Z		Radstand vorne	Radstand hinten
3,50 m		1,16 m	1,14 m
A			
0,88 m			

Wendekreis 9,75 m, ungefähres Gewicht 597 kg

LIEFERBARE FARBKOMBINATIONEN

Karosserie	Innenausstattung	Verdeck
tartan rot	rot oder schwarz	rot
Riviera blau	blau	blau
old English weiß	rot	grau
old English weiß	schwarz	schwarz
Taubengrau	grau	grau
schwarz	rot	schwarz
British Racing grün	schwarz	schwarz
Fiesta gelb	schwarz	schwarz

(Änderungen vorbehalten)

Diese Veröffentlichung bedeutet kein Angebot. Technische und preisliche Änderungen bleiben jederzeit und ohne Ankündigung vorbehalten. Es gelten die Verkaufs- und Garantiebestimmungen der Austin Motor Export Corporation Ltd. Die Preisliste ist separat.

Das Faltverdeck des Sprite ist so gearbeitet, daß es rundum dicht abschließt, und die Benutzung der Kurbelfenster wie bei einer Limousine gewährleistet ist. Die Innenausstattung des Sprite MK II ist sehr luxuriös und umfangreich.

Alle Instrumente und Bedienungsknöpfe sind übersichtlich und in bequemer Reichweite des Fahrers angeordnet. Die Heizung und ein eventuell nachträglich eingebautes Radio lassen sich leicht bedienen. Ein elektrischer Tourenzähler mit Ladekontrolle gehört zur Serienausstattung.

Die Instrumente sind zur besseren Kontrolle unmittelbar vor dem Fahrer angebracht, während sich auf der Beifahrerseite unterhalb des Armaturenbrettes ein Ablagefach befindet.

Bei der Ausstattung des Innenraumes wurde Kunstleder verwendet. Sitze, Türverkleidungen und Armaturenbrett sind mit diesem verschleißfesten Material bezogen, welches leicht sauber gehalten werden kann, da es abwaschbar ist.

A new instrument panel, cranked windows, and spoked wheels offered as an option tried to deny the kinship to the "Frogeye."

Export Equipment

To satisfy the demands of the world market, the standard equipment of the Austin Healey Sprite Mk. III "Export" includes the following items:

Front and rear bumpers with overriders, electric tachometer, windshield washer system, fresh-air heating, adjustable seats, seat covers, steering lock.

The Export model is delivered in the following variations at no extra charge:

Right-or left-hand steering, odometer in miles or kilometers, headlights and directional lights corresponding to the country's regulations.

Special equipment at extra charge:

Radio, laminated glass windshield, locking filler cap, cigarette lighter, two-tone horn, rear seat cushion, luggage rack, coconut mats, wooden steering wheel, radiator blind, spoked wheels, transverse stabilizer, flasher.

This publication does not constitute an offer. Technical and price changes may be made at any time without advance notice. The sales and guarantee conditions of the Austin Motor Export Corporation Ltd. apply. The price list is separate.

The folding top of the Sprite is so made that it is watertight all around, and the use of the cranked windows is guaranteed as in a sedan. The interior decor of the Sprite Mark II is very luxurious and inclusive.

All instruments and controls are easy for the driver to see and reach. The heating, and a radio that may be installed later, are easy to control. An electric tachometer with controls is part of the standard equipment. For better observation, the instruments are grouped in front of the driver, while a glove compartment is located under the dashboard on the passenger side.

Imitation leather was used to decorate the interior. Seats, door coverings and dashboard are covered with this impervious material, which can be kept clean easily, as it is washable.

In 1966 the last version of the Austin Healey Sprite appeared in the form of the Mark IV. With the rally-tested 1275-cc motor of the Mini-Cooper, it produced 65 HP, and its top speed was somewhere over 150 kph. The Mark IV had come a long way from the original form of the Sprite . . .

Sprite Mark IV . . . that means technically advanced and matured, modern and practical design, safety and elegance, reliable and stable, in short: a true English sports car.

SPRITE MK IV

Sprite MK IV . . . das bedeutet: technisch fortschrittlich und ausgereift, moderne und zweckmäßige Formgestaltung, Sicherheit und Eleganz, zuverlässig und stabil, kurz gesagt: ein echter englischer Sportwagen.

The first brochure for the Austin Healey Sprite Mark IV, which was also issued in German in 1966. The illustrations show only right-hand-drive cars, though.

For little money, a well-equipped little roadster!

Für Alle, welche jung — oder jung geblieben sind, bietet der Sprite die Erfüllung vieler Wünsche. Da er ein Sportwagen aus echtem Schrot und Korn ist, macht er das Autofahren zur Freude und Entspannung. Seit der erste Sprite 1958 auf den Markt kam, hat besonders die Jugend aller Kontinente von ihm Besitz ergriffen.

Bei der Entwicklung des AUSTIN Healey Sprite haben wir besonderen Wert darauf gelegt, einen echten Sportwagen zu einem Preis anzubieten, der für breiteste Schichten erschwinglich ist. Aber damit nicht genug, der Sprite ist außerdem billig in der Unterhaltung und im Kundendienst. Vergleichen Sie ihn mit anderen Sportwagen (aber echten) und Sie werden erstaunt sein!
AUSTIN Healey Sprite MK IV . . . ein kleiner Sportwagen — aber mit den Fahreigenschaften eines großen Roadsters.

Der Sprite wird in der Standardausführung mit Scheibenrädern und gegen Aufpreis mit Speichenrädern geliefert. Die Abbildung zeigt ein Speichenrad.

Da der Sprite ein bekannt sicheres Fahrzeug ist, kann er schnell und spritzig gefahren werden. Gute Straßenlage, moderne Bremsanlage, stabile Verarbeitung und noch vieles mehr haben den Sprite weltberühmt gemacht.

For all who are—or have remained—young, the Sprite offers the fulfillment of many wishes. Since it is a genuine sports car, it makes driving fun and relaxation. Since the first Sprite came on the market in 1958, the youth of all continents has particularly taken to it.
Since the Sprite is known as a safe vehicle, it can be driven with speed and spirit. Good roadholding, modern brakes, stable construction and much more have made the Sprite world-famous.
In developing the Austin Healey Sprite, we have put particular emphasis on offering a genuine sports car at a price that is affordable at the broadest levels. But that is not enough. The Sprite is also economical to maintain and have serviced. Compare it with other sports cars (but genuine ones) and you will be astonished! Austin Healey Sprite Mark IV . . . a little sports car—but with the driving characteristics of a big roadster.
The Sprite is available with standard disc wheels and available with spoked wheels at extra charge. The picture shows a spoked wheel.

...a genuine roadster
...a genuine roadster
WITH CONVERTIBLE TOP

Whether they are Austin bodywork builders or constructors, they have all worked for months to develop a perfect sports car with the conveniences of a sedan.

It was made sure that the body-formed bucket seats are not located over the axles, the dashboard is easy to see, the interior is made of durable, washable synthetic material, the floor is covered with durable and tasteful carpeting, both seats are adjustable, all colors blend well with each other.

The instruments are located where they are easy to read, directly in front of the driver.

The spare wheel, as the illustration shows, lies at the bottom of the trunk. Yet the trunk is big enough to hold small luggage.

A few twists suffice to raise or lower the convertible top. The top folds easily and disappears behind the seats.

The fabric of the top is canvas mixed with plastic and is absolutely watertight. With the top up, the Sprite thus offers the same comfort as a sedan. The big rear window in the roof, as well as the big bowed windshield, provide an ideal view.

At an extra charge, a seat cover can be obtained. With it, the interior can be completely or only half covered (see the lower middle picture). All doors can be locked by separate locks.

Ob Karosseriebauer oder Konstrukteure von Austin, alle haben monatelang daran gearbeitet, einen perfekten Sportwagen mit den Bequemlichkeiten einer Limousine zu entwickeln.

Es wurde darauf geachtet, daß sich die körpergerechten Schalensitze nicht über den Achsen befinden, das Armaturenbrett ist übersichtlich gestaltet, das Interieur besteht aus strapazierfähigem, abwaschbaren Kunststoff, der Boden ist mit einem haltbaren und geschmackvollen Teppich ausgelegt, beide Sitze sind verstellbar, alle Farben sind gut miteinander abgestimmt.

Direkt vor dem Fahrer sind die Instrumente leicht ablesbar angebracht.

Das Reserverad liegt, wie die Abbildung zeigt, auf dem Boden des Kofferraumes. Dennoch ist der Kofferraum groß genug, um Kleingepäck zu verstauen.

Wenige Handgriffe genügen, um das Kabrioverdeck zu öffnen bzw. zu schließen. Das Verdeck faltet sich mühelos und verschwindet hinter den Sitzen.

...ein echter *Roadster*
MIT KABRIOVERDECK

Das Verdecktuch besteht aus Segeltuch gemischt mit Kunststoff und schließt absolut dicht ab. Im geschlossenen Zustand bietet daher der Sprite den gleichen Komfort wie eine Limousine. Das große Heckfenster im Verdeck sowie die große gewölbte Windschutzscheibe gewähren ideale Sicht.

Gegen Aufpreis kann eine Sitzabdeckung geliefert werden. Damit kann der Innenraum ganz oder auch nur halb abgedeckt werden (s. Bild unten Mitte). Alle Türen sind abschließbar durch separate Türschlösser.

In terms of equipment, practically nothing had changed from the forerunner Mark III model. Basically, the owner of a Mark IV lacked nothing, compared with the original 1958 version.

Open the engine hood . . .
AUSTIN HEALEY SPRITE
presents the new 1275 cc BMC "A" motor
STRONGERFASTERMORE ELASTIC

The secret of the Sprite Mark IV is its heart. Open the engine hood and before you lies the new BMC "A" motor. Two SU carburetors, double valve springs, strengthened clutch, higher torque, more horsepower, these are just some of the factors that make the Sprite Mark IV so interesting. The gearbox is synchronized, with the third gear ratio chosen to provide the greatest acceleration.

In the Mark IV, not only did the body and chassis cooperate to give the feeling of a real sports car, but nothing more was lacking in terms of engine power either.

Öffnen Sie die Motorhaube . . .

AUSTIN HEALEY SPRITE

präsentiert den neuen 1275 ccm BMC „A" Motor

STÄRKER

SCHNELLER

ELASTISCHER

Das Geheimnis des Sprite MK IV ist sein Herz. Öffnen Sie die Motorhaube und vor Ihnen liegt der neue BMC-„A"-Motor. Zwei SU-Vergaser, doppelte Ventilfedern, verstärkte Kupplung, höheres Drehmoment, mehr PS, dies sind nur einige der Faktoren, die den Sprite MK IV so interessant machen. Das Getriebe ist synchronisiert, wobei der dritte Gang so übersetzt wurde, daß hier die größte Beschleunigung erreicht werden kann.

Schnelle Wagen brauchen gute Bremsen. Hierauf haben wir besonderen Wert gelegt. Große Scheibenbremsen vorn (∅ 209 mm) und Trommelbremsen hinten gewährleisten ein Maximum an Sicherheit.
Die hervorragende Straßenlage des Sprite wird durch seine Radaufhängung erreicht. Vorn: Schraubenfedern, hydraulische Stoßdämpfer, Einzelradaufhängung, obere Tragarme direkt mit den Stoßdämpfern verbunden, tiefliegender Schwerpunkt. Hinten: halbelliptische Blattfedern und hydraulische Stoßdämpfer.

Hypoidverzahnte Hinterachse: das bedeutet ruhiger Lauf und beste Straßenlage.

Die Zahnstangenlenkung ist robust und direkt, für einen Sportwagen von größter Wichtigkeit. Nur 2⅓ Umdrehungen des Lenkrades sind zum Volleinschlag der Räder notwendig. Das Lenkrad ist sportlich und hat einen Durchmesser von nur 400 mm.

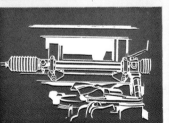

Im September 1959 wurden mit dem Sprite auf der Rekordstrecke von Utah/USA verschiedene internationale Geschwindigkeitsrekorde aufgestellt. Dabei wurden nicht weniger als 50 amerikanische und 15 internationale Rekorde erzielt. Auf einer Marathonstrecke von 2664 km wurde ein Geschwindigkeitsdurchschnitt von 222 km/h ermittelt, ohne daß an dem Fahrzeug Schäden aufgetreten sind.
Im April 1960 gewannen die AUSTIN Healey Sprite eine der schwersten Rallyes in Irland. Alle ersten 6 Plätze wurden gewonnen sowie im Gesamtklassement der dritte Platz. Seit dieser Zeit haben die Sprite auf allen Rennplätzen der Welt beachtliche Erfolge errungen. Ein anderer großer Sprite-Erfolg war das 24 Std. Rennen von Le Mans 1960 und 1965. Hier gewannen die Sprite in der Klasse von 851 ccm bis 1100 ccm mit einer Durchschnittsgeschwindigkeit von 136,9 km/h. Auf der internationalen Rallye Liege-Rom-Liege 1960 dritter Platz im Gesamtklassement und Klassensieger. Von 82 gestarteten Wagen erreichten bei dieser schweren Prüfung nur 13 das Ziel. In Sebring konnten die AUSTIN Healey Sprite ihre Erfolge fortsetzen.

Rekordwagen AUSTIN HEALEY

1961 belegten die Sprite in der Klasse 6 den ersten, zweiten und dritten Platz während beim 4-Stunden-Rennen unter 1000 ccm alle ersten Plätze gewonnen wurden.

All diese Erfolge sind ein Beweis, daß der AUSTIN Healey Sprite zu den besten Sportwagen gehört, welche heute auf dem Markt sind. Modern in der Konstruktion und hervorragend in der Verarbeitung ist er das Produkt bester englischer Wertarbeit.

Hypoid-geared rear axle: that means quieter runnin[g] and best roadholding.
The rack-and-pinion steering is robust and direct, [of] greatest importance in a sports car. Only two and on[e] third revolutions of the steering wheel from block [to] block are necessary. The steering wheel is sporty an[d] has a diameter of only 400 mm.
Fast cars need good brakes. We have given speci[al] emphasis to this. Large front disc brakes (209 m[m] diameter) and rear drum brakes provide a maximum [of] safety.
The excellent roadholding of the Sprite is attained b[y] its suspension. Front: coil springs, hydraulic shoc[k] absorbers, independent suspension, upper carryin[g] arms directly linked to the shock absorbers, low-lyin[g] center of gravity. Rear: semi-elliptic leaf springs an[d] hydraulic shock absorbers.
In September of 1959 the Sprite set various internationa[l] speed records on the record course in Utah, USA. In th[e] process, no fewer than 50 American and 15 internationa[l] records were set. In a marathon run of 2664 km, a[n] average speed of 222 kph was maintained without a[ny] damage to the vehicle.
In April of 1960 the Austin Healey Sprite won one [of] the most difficult rallies in Ireland. All the first si[x] places were won, as well as third place in the genera[l] classification. Since this time the Sprite has gaine[d] noteworthy victories on all the world's racecourse[s.] Another great Sprite victory was the 24 Hour Race of L[e] Mans in 1960 and 1965. Here the Sprite won the clas[s] from 851 to 1100 cc with an average speed of 136.9 kph[.] In the 1960 international Liège-Rome-Liège Rall[y] third place in the general classification and a clas[s] victory. Of 82 cars that started, only 13 reached th[e] finish line of this tough test. At Sebring the Austi[n] Healey Sprites were able to continue their victories.
In 1961 the Sprite took the first, second and third plac[e] in Class 6, while winning all first places in the fou[r] hour race under 1000 cc.
All of these victories are an indication that the Austi[n] Healey Sprite ranks among the best sports cars that [are] on the market today. Modern in construction an[d] outstanding in workmanship, it is the product of th[e] best English quality work.

AUSTIN HEALEY Speed Record Car

The already long list of international sporting victories and record runs was lengthened again and again.

ECHNICAL DATA

otor: Four-cylinder overhead-valve motor, bore: 70.63 m, stroke: 81.33 mm, displacement: 1275 cc; 65 HP at 6000 m; maximum torque 10 kg/meter at 3000 rpm; mpression 8.81.

ubrication: Oil pump driven by camshaft, pressure lubri- ion with mainstream filter, oil-pan capacity approx. 3.9 ers.

ooling: Pressure cooling with centrifugal water pump, diator, thermostat. Cooling water capacity: approx. 5.7 ers.

arburetors: Two SU HS 2 downdraft carburetors, air filter th paper filter.

el Pump: SU fuel pump, electric. Tank capacity: approx. 3 liters.

nition: Coil, distributor with automatic setting.

hassis:

lutch: Membrane clutch, diameter 160 mm, hydraulically tivated by hanging pedal.

ears: Four-speed gearbox, synchronized in 2nd, 3rd and 4th ars. Ratios: 1st gear: 3.2:1, 2nd gear: 1.916:1, 3rd gear: 357:1, 4th gear: 1.1, reverse gear: 4.120:1. Stick shift with ntrally located stick shift. Oil capacity, approx. 1.4 liters. anual transmission (insert above).

riveshaft: Open shaft with needle bearings and cross links.

ear Axle: Hypoid-geared rear axle with plate and bevel ar. Ratio: 4.22:1. Oil capacity approx. 1 liter. Ratios: 1st ar: 13.5:1, 2nd gear: 8.08:1, 3rd gear: 5.72:1, 4th gear: 4.22:1, verse gear: 17.39:1.

uspension and springs: Front: independent suspension ith coil springs and triangular links. Rear: semi-elliptical af springs. Front and rear hydraulic shock absorbers.

akes: Hydraulic four-wheel brakes, activated by hanging dal. Hand brake works on the rear wheels via a mpensator. Front disc brake diameter 209 mm. Rear drum akes, 178 x 31.8 mm.

heels and Tires: Pressed steel disc wheels with ventilation ts. Tires: 5.20 x 13 Dunlop Tubeless.

ectrical System: 12-volt generator and starter. 43 A/h ttery. Foot dimmer switch, combined stop, tail and rectional lights, indicator lights for ignition, battery arge, high beams, oil-filter dirt. Dual windshield wipers, mbined ignition and steering lock, directional light vitch on the steering column, turns off automatically.

struments: Combined speedometer and odometer, daily lometer, fuel gauge, electric tachometer, combined water- mperature and oil-pressure indicator.

eering: Rack and pinion steering. Three-spoke steering heel, diameter 400 mm. Turning circle 9.79 meters.

dy: Two-door sports car with two bucket seats, motor od attached by hinges at the rear, with lock released from side, locking luggage compartment. Large arched indshield in aluminum frame. Cranked door windows th separate vent windows. Plastic inside coverings. Floor vered with carpeting. Adjustable seats with foam rubber pholstery, attachments for seat belts. Locking doors. Spare heel in trunk. convertible top made of vinyl plastic. Inside irror adjustable vertically. chromed bumpers with verriders. Windshield washer system. Fresh air heating. eering lock.

an extra charge, the car can be delivered with oil cooler, at covers, spoked wheels, Dunlop SP tires d flasher lights. For additional accessories, ask your USTIN dealer.

he manufacturer reserves the right to make model and rice changes without advance notice. This brochure is not offer and not binding. For prices, see the separate list. xclusive Austin importer:

Technical data from an Austin Healey Mark IV brochure of 1966.

Austin Healey

SPRITE
MK IV

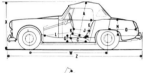

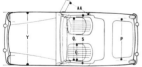

MASSE UND GEWICHTE:

AA	A	C	E
0,66 m	0,90 m	0,48 m	0,48 m
G	**J (min.)**	**J (max.)**	**K**
0,22 m	0,35 m	0,44 m	0,13 m
L (min.)	**L (max.)**	**N**	**O**
1,04 m	1,13 m	0,40 m	0,70 m
P	**Q1**	**Q2**	**S**
1,07 m	0,43 m	1,12 m	1,23 m
W	**X** Verdeck geöffnet 1,24 m	**Y**	**Z**
2,03 m		1,40 m	3,50 m
Bodenfreiheit 0,13 m	**Spur vorn** 1,18 m	**Spur hinten** 1,14 m	**Gewicht** 686 kg

TECHNISCHE DATEN

MOTOR: Vierzylinder, obengesteuerter Motor, Bohrung: 70,63 mm; Hub: 81,33 mm; Zylinderinhalt: 1275 ccm; 65 PS bei 6000 U/min.; max. Drehmoment: 10 kg/m bei 3000 U/min.; Verdichtung 8,8 : 1.

SCHMIERUNG: Ölpumpe durch Nockenwelle angetrieben, Druckumlaufschmierung mit Filter im Hauptstrom, Ölwanneninhalt ca. 3,9 Ltr.

KÜHLUNG: Druckkühler mit Zentrifugal-Wasserpumpe, Ventilator, Thermostat, Kühlwasserinhalt ca. 5,7 Ltr.

VERGASER: Zwei SU-HS 2 Fallstromvergaser, Luftfilter mit Papierfilter.

BENZINPUMPE: SU-Benzinpumpe elektrisch, Tankinhalt ca. 27,3 Ltr.

ZÜNDUNG: Zündspule, Zündverteiler mit automatischer Einstellung.

CHASSIS:

Kupplung: Membranenkupplung ⌀ 160 mm, hydraulisch betätigt durch hängende Pedale.

Getriebe: Vierganggetriebe, synchronisiert im 2., 3. und 4. Gang. Übersetzung 1. Gang: 3,2 : 1, 2. Gang: 1,916 : 1, 3. Gang: 1,357 : 1, 4. Gang: 1 : 1, Rückwärtsgang: 4,120 : 1, Stockschaltung mit zentral gelegenem kurzen Schalthebel, Ölinhalt ca. 1,4 Ltr.

Kardanwelle: offenliegende Welle mit Nadellagern und Kreuzgelenken.

Hinterachse: hypoidverzahnte Hinterachse mit Teller- und Kegelrad, Übersetzung 4,22 : 1. Ölinhalt ca. 1 Ltr. Übersetzungen: 1. Gang: 13,5 : 1, 2. Gang: 8,08 : 1, 3. Gang: 5,72 : 1, 4. Gang: 4,22 : 1, Rückwärtsgang: 17,39 : 1.

Radaufhängung und Federung: Vorn: Unabhängige Einzelradaufhängung mit Schraubenfedern und Dreieckslenker. Hinten: Halbelliptische Blattfedern. Hydraulische Stoßdämpfer vorn und hinten.

Bremsen: Hydraulische Vierradbremse betätigt durch hängende Pedale, Handbremse wirkt auf die Hinterräder durch Kompensator. Scheibenbremsen vorn ⌀ 209 mm, Trommelbremsen hinten 178 mm × 31,8 mm.

Räder und Reifen: Preßstahl-Scheibenräder mit Ventilationsschlitzen, Reifen: 5,20 × 13 Dunlop schlauchlos.

ELEKTRISCHE ANLAGE: 12-Volt-Lichtmaschine und Anlasser, 43 A/h Batterie, Fußabblendschalter, kombinierte Stopp-, Schluß- und Blinkleuchten, Kontrolleuchten für Zündung, Ladekontrolle, Fernlicht, Ölfilterverschmutzung, Doppelte Scheibenwischer, kombiniertes Zünd- und Lenkschloß, selbstrückstellender Blinkerschalter an der Lenksäule.

INSTRUMENTE: kombinierter Geschwindigkeits- und Kilometerzähler, Kilometerzähler mit Tageszählwerk, Benzinuhr, elektrischer Tourenzähler, kombinierte Kühlwassertemperatur- und Öldruckanzeige.

Lenkung: Zahnstangenlenkung, Dreispeichenlenkrad ⌀ 400 mm, Wendekreis 9,79 m.

KAROSSERIE: Zweitüriger Sportwagen mit zwei Schalensitzen, hinten in Scharniere aufgehängte Motorhaube mit Haubenschloß zum Öffnen von innen, abschließbarer Kofferraum. Gebogene große Windschutzscheibe in Aluminiumrahmen, Kurbelfenster an den Türen mit separaten Ausstellfenstern. Innenverkleidung aus Kunststoff, Fußboden mit Teppichmaterial ausgelegt. Verstellbare, schaumgummigepolsterte Sitze, Vorrichtungen für Sitzgurte. Abschließbare Türen. Reserverad liegt im Kofferraum. Kabrioverdeck aus Vinyl-Kunststoff. Senkrecht verstellbarer Innenspiegel. Verchromte Stoßstangen mit Hörnern. Scheibenwaschanlage, Frischluftheizung, Lenkschloß.

Gegen Aufpreis kann der Wagen mit Ölkühler, Sitzabdeckung, Querstabilisator, Speichenräder „Dunlop SP-Reifen" und Lichthupe geliefert werden. Nach weiteren Zubehörfragen Sie bitte Ihren AUSTIN-Händler.

Der Hersteller behält sich das Recht vor, ohne Vorankündigung Modell und Preisänderungen vorzunehmen. Dieser Prospekt ist kein Angebot und unverbindlich. Preise siehe separate Liste.

Austin-Alleinimporteur:

A. BRÜGGEMANN & CO. GMBH.
DÜSSELDORF, Harffstraße 53
Filiale: HEIDELBERG, Hebelstraße 12

THE BRITISH MOTOR COMPANY LIMITED
BMC EXPORT SALES LIMITED

LONGBRIDGE — BIRMINGHAM — ENGLAND

Publ. Nr. 2390 D

A new level of excitement and luxury

Since its introduction in 1958, the Austin-Healey Sprite has been raced and rallied with enormous success the world over. But undoubtedly its greatest achievement has been in providing the ordinary motorist with maximum fun and performance for minimum money.

Now, with new front grille and restyled interior trim, this latest version of the Sprite is even more attractive and luxurious.

Equally at home in the hands of the novice or hardened enthusiast alike, the Austin-Healey Sprite Mk. IV offers the highest possible standard of safety and road-worthiness, superb reliability and remarkable economy, coupled with the sheer pleasure of owning a car that has achieved universal acclaim.

The Austin Healey Sprite became more and more modern and at the same time more suited to American taste in its last years of production. In this 1969 catalog one sees clearly the not exactly beautiful new radiator grille.

A short, remote-control gear lever permits quick, positive changes in the best sports car tradition.

Luxury in full measure with restfully upholstered reclining bucket seats. Seat belts must be fitted by your dealer.

Padded fascia with full instrumentation to keep you in tune with the performance! Racy, 3-spoke steering wheel with simulated leather-bound rim. Radio at extra cost.

Aerodynamic styling with the safety of all-steel mono-construction.

There's plenty of room for luggage in the Sprite's lockable boot.

Behind those sporty 'Rostyle' front wheels are disc brakes for dead-in-line, fade-free stopping. Rack and pinion steering and tough suspension help the Sprite through the lightest turns.

Race-proven 1275 c.c. engine with twin S.U. carburetters delivers performance with economy.

Easily raised/lowered,quick-stowing integral hood. Efficient heater/demister is standard.

Technically, nothing important changed any more to
the end of production.

Dimensions

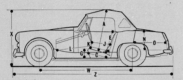

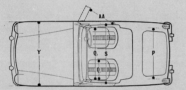

		English	Metric
Front seat head room ..	A	35·5 in.	90 cm.
Front seat cushion depth	C	19 in.	48 cm.
Front seat squab height above cushion	E	19 in.	48 cm.
Front seat cushion height above floor ..	G	8·5 in.	22 cm.
Steering-wheel to squab—max.	J	17·25 in.	44 cm.
Steering-wheel to squab—min.	J	13·75 in.	35 cm.
Steering-wheel to cushion	K	5 in.	13 cm.
Front seat leg reach—max.	L	44·5 in.	113 cm.
Front seat leg reach—min.	L	41 in.	104 cm.
Luggage boot height ..	N	15·5 in.	40 cm.
Luggage boot depth ..	O	27·5 in.	70 cm.
Luggage boot width ..	P	42 in.	107 cm.
Front seat cushion width—individual	Q1	17 in.	43 cm.
Front seat cushion—overall width	Q2	44·25 in.	112 cm.
Width between front doors—max.	S	48·5 in.	123 cm.
Wheelbase	W	80 in.	203 cm.
Overall height (hood up)	X	48·625 in.	124 cm.
Overall width	Y	54·875 in.	140 cm.
Overall length with over-riders	Z	137·375 in.	350 cm.
Front door entry width ..	AA	26 in.	66 cm.
Ground clearance		5 in.	12·7 cm.
Approx. weight		1,575 lb.	714 kg.

Specification

ENGINE: Four cylinders, overhead valves; bore 2·78 in. (70·61 mm.); stroke 3·2 in. (81·28 mm.); cubic capacity 77·9 cu. in. (1275 c.c.); b.h.p. 65 at 6,000 r.p.m., maximum torque 72 lb. ft. at 3,000 r.p.m.; compression ratio 8·8 : 1 (8 : 1 available if required).

LUBRICATION: Concentric pump, driven by camshaft, forces filtered oil to all working parts; sump capacity 6 pints (3·41 litres) plus 1 pint (0·57 litre) for full-flow filter.

COOLING: Pressurized radiator with centrifugal pump and fan; circulation controlled by thermostat; approximate capacity 6 pints (3·4 litres).

FUEL SYSTEM: Twin S.U. type HS2 semi-downdraught carburetters, fitted with paper element type air cleaners; S.U. electric fuel pump; fuel capacity 6 gallons (27·28 litres).

IGNITION: Coil, and distributor with automatic and vacuum control.

CLUTCH: Diaphragm-spring type; 6·5 in. (0·16 m.) diameter; hydraulically operated by pendent pedal.

GEARBOX: Four speed, with baulk-ring synchromesh on second, third, and top speeds; ratios—first 3·2, second 1·916, third 1·357, top 1·00, reverse 4·114 : 1; remote-control gear lever centrally mounted on floor; oil capacity 2·33 pints (1·33 litres).

PROPELLER SHAFT: Open, with needle-roller-bearing universal joints; sliding splines in gearbox.

REAR AXLE: Three-quarter-floating with hypoid bevel crown wheel and pinion; ratio 3·9 : 1, oil capacity 1·75 pints (1 litre); overall gear ratios—first 12·5, second 7·5, third 5·3, top 3·9, reverse 16·04 : 1.

STEERING: Rack and pinion; three-spoke, 15·5 in. (0·40 m.) diameter steering-wheel. Turning circle: left 32 ft. 1·5 in. (9·79 m.), right 31 ft. 2·5 in. (9·51 m.). Track: front 3 ft. 10·312 in. (1·18 m.), rear 3 ft. 8·75 in. (1·14 m.).

SUSPENSION: Front—independent with coil springs and wishbones; rear—semi-elliptic leaf springs. Hydraulic shock absorbers front and rear.

BRAKES: Four-wheel hydraulic, operated by pendent pedal. Pull-up hand brake lever operates on rear wheels through compensator. Dimensions: front 8·25 in. (209 mm.) diameter disc; rear 7 in. (178 mm.) diameter drum.

WHEELS AND TYRES: Pressed-steel, Rostyle wheels with four-stud fixing; 5·20—13 four-ply tubeless tyres.

ELECTRICAL: 12-volt generator and starter motor; 43-amp.-hr. capacity battery at 20-hour rate; double-dipping headlamps; sidelamps combined with front amber flashers; twin stop/tail lamps, red reflectors and amber flashers combined in one unit; twin rear number-plate lamps; warning lamps to indicate flashers working, generator not charging, and headlamps high-beam position; twin windscreen wipers; twin horns; combined ignition and starting switch; single lever on steering-column controls horn, headlamp flasher, dip-switch and self-cancelling flashers; twin reversing lamps.

INSTRUMENTS: Speedometer with trip and total mileage recorder; fuel gauge; combined oil pressure and water temperature gauges; electric tachometer.

BODYWORK: Two-door, two-seater sports car of all-steel mono-construction. Rear hinged bonnet with lock controlled from inside car. Luggage compartment has lockable lid. Curved, zone-toughened glass windscreen in black frame; wind-down door windows with hinged ventilators. Interior trim in leathercloth. Both seats adjustable fore and aft, having foam-rubber cushions, with rubberized-hair. Adjustable squabs. Seat wearing surfaces upholstered in knit-backed expanded vinyl. In-built fittings for seat belts. Floor covered with carpet. Each door is fitted with a recessed internal release lever and has external push-button handles and locks. Spare wheel secured horizontally in luggage compartment. Integral vinyl-coated fabric hood with cover. Interior rear-view anti-dazzle mirror mounted on centre screen rod. Full-width front bumper and rear quarter bumpers with over-riders. Windscreen washer. Fresh-air heater.

OPTIONAL EXTRAS: Tonneau cover; wire wheels; anti-roll bar; oil cooler; laminated windscreen; hard top; radial-ply tyres.

These specification details do not apply to any particular vehicle which is supplied or offered for sale. The manufacturers reserve the right to vary their specification with or without notice and at such times and in such manner as they think fit. Major as well as minor changes may be involved. Therefore, although every effort is made to ensure the accuracy of the particulars contained in this brochure, neither the Company nor the Distributor or Dealer by whom this publication is issued shall be liable for any inaccuracy in any circumstances whatsoever. Consult the Dealer with whom your order is placed for details of the specification of any particular vehicle. This publication shall not constitute in any circumstances whatsoever an offer by the Company to any person. All sales are made by the Distributor or Dealer concerned subject to and with the benefit of the standard Conditions of Sale and Warranty given by the Distributor or Dealer, copies of which may be obtained from him on request.

BRITISH LEYLAND (AUSTIN-MORRIS) LIMITED
LONGBRIDGE, BIRMINGHAM, ENGLAND

Printed letterpress by The Nuffield Press Limited, Cowley, Oxford, England 23/180 (26810) 10/69—100m. Publication No. 2691

BRITISH
LEYLAND

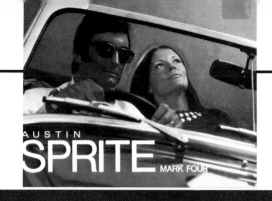

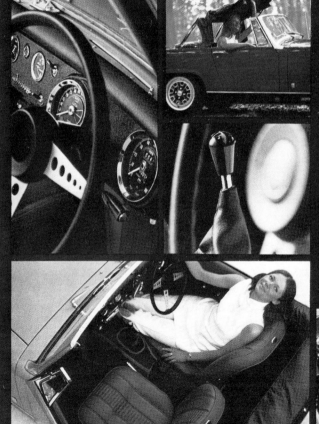

the budget-priced sports car that's got the lot

Small in size and cost, big in heart and spirit, the Mk IV Austin Sprite puts the fun and excitement back into motoring.

Here is everything the enthusiast-driver looks for in a car—surging twin-carb power, crisp control responses, superb roadholding, rally-trim styling, full instrumentation, powerful, fade-free braking. . . .

From its dramatic Rostyle road wheels to its quick-stowing, weatherproof hood, the Sprite is rich in sporting character.

Padded fascia, with full instrume Racy, 3-spoke steering wheel with si leather-bound rim.

Easily raised/lowered, quick-stowing hood.

A short, remote-control gear lever give positive changes in the best sports ca tion.

The last brochure for the Austin Healey Sprite, printed in December of 1970. A jolly little high-performance sports car for many, a caricature of the old Sprite for some. Production ended something over a year later.

in full measure, with restfully ered, rake-adjusting bucket seats

roven 1275 c.c. engine with twin rburetters delivers performance with y.

plenty of room for luggage in the e boot.

Austin Healey Four Cylinder

Model	100 BN 1	100 BN 2	100 S	100 M
Years made	1952-1955	1955-1956	1954-1956	1955-1956
Motor	in-line 4	in-line 4	in-line 4	in-line 4
Bore x stroke	87.3 x 111.1 = 2660 cc			
Compression	7.5 : 1	7.5 : 1	8.3 : 1	8.1 : 1
HP at rpm	90/4000	90/4000	132/4700	110/4550
Valves	overhead	overhead	overhead	overhead
Lubrication	pressure	pressure	pressure	pressure
Cooling	water	water	water	water
Carburetors	2 SU	2 SU	2 SU	2 SU
Gears	4 + R	4 + R + OD	4 + R + OD	4 + R + OD
Brakes	drum	drum	disc	disc
Chassis	box-frame	box-frame	box-frame	box-frame
Wheelbase	2250 mm	2250 mm	2250 mm	2250 mm
Track	1262 mm	1262 mm	1280 mm	1262 mm
Tire size	5.90 x 15	5.90 x 15	5.50 x 15	5.90 x 15
Top speed	170 kph	170 kph	200 kph	188 kph
Number made	10,688	3,924	55	1,159

Austin Healey Six Cylinder

Model	100/6 BN 4	100/6 BN 6	3000 BN 7	3000 Mk. II	3000 Mk. III
Years made	1956	1957-1959	1959-1961	1962-1964	1964-1968
Motor	in-line 6	in-line 6	in-line 6	in-line 6	in-line 6
Bore x stroke	79.4 x 88.9 = 2639 cc	79.4 x 88.9 = 2639 cc	83.3 x 88.9 = 2912 cc	83.3 x 88.9 = 2912 cc	83.3 x 88.9 = 2912 cc
Compression	8.25 : 1	8.7 : 1	9.1 : 1	9.0 : 1	9.0 : 1
HP at rpm	100/4650	117/5000	124/4600	132/4750	148/5250
Valves	overhead	overhead	overhead	overhead	overhead
Lubrication	pressure	pressure	pressure	pressure	pressure
Cooling	water	water	water	water	water
Carburetors	2 SU	2 SU	2 SU	3 SU	2 SU
Gears	4 + R + OD	4 + R + OD	4 + R + OD	4 + R + OD	4 + R + OD
Brakes	drum	drum	front disc/rear drum	front disc/rear drum	front disc/rear drum
Chassis	box-frame	box-frame	box-frame	box-frame	box frame
Wheelbase	2300 mm	2300 mm	2300 mm	2300 mm	2300 mm
Track	1350 mm	1350 mm	1350 mm	1350 mm	1350 mm
Tire size	5.90 x 15	5.90 x 15	5.90 x 15	5.90 x 15	5.90 x 15
Top speed	168 kph	170 kph	182 kph	180 kph	195 kph
Number made	10,286	4,150	13,650	11,543	17,712

No need for apprehension as the storm clouds gather, for the Austin Healey '100-Six' equipped with a 'Hard Top' is completely weatherproof.

In 1961 this folding brochure appeared, its upper half covering the picture of the open car. Advertising text: "Thus you change your Austin Healey 3000 into a chic sport sedan.

Healey | "3000" | Wet or fine . . . . keep pace with the mood of the weather by the use of a detachable 'Hard Top'.

Austin Healey Sprite

Model	Sprite Mk. I	Sprite Mk. II	Sprite Mk. II/1100	Sprite Mk. III	Sprite Mk. IV
Years made	1958-1961	1961-1962	1962-1964	1964-1966	1966-1972
Motor	in-line 4	in-line 4	in-line 4	in-line 4	in-line 4
Bore x stroke	62.9 x 76.2 = 948 cc	62.9 x 76.2 = 948 cc	64.6 x 83.7 = 1098 cc	64.6 x 83.7 = 1098 cc	70.6 x 81.3 = 1275 cc
Compression	8.75 : 1	9.0 : 1	8.9 : 1	9.0 : 1	9.0 : 1
HP at rpm	46/5200	49/5500	56/5750	59/5750	65/6000
Valves	overhead	overhead	overhead	overhead	overhead
Lubrication	pressure	pressure	pressure	pressure	pressure
Cooling	water	water	water	water	water
Carburetors	2 SU	2 SU	2 SU	2 SU	2 SU
Gears	4 + R	4 + R	4 + R	4 + R	4 + R
Brakes	drum	drum	drum	front disc/rear drum	front disc/rear drum
Chassis	box-frame	box-frame	box-frame	box-frame	box frame
Wheelbase	2000 mm	2000 mm	2000 mm	2000 mm	2000 mm
Track	1018 mm	1043 mm	1043 mm	1043 mm	1043 mm
Tire size	5.20 x 13	5.20 x 13	5.20 x 13	5.20 x 13	5.20 x 13
Top speed	133 kph	140 kph	145 kph	148 kph	152 kph
Number made	48,999	19.285	11,215	25,905	22,170

The Austin Healey in the Press

The Austin Healey 100, already a well-known sales success in the USA, was still something exotic to the German drivers of the mid-Fifties, and for most of them an unattainable dream car when, in 1954, the magazine *Motor Rundschau* got the chance to test one briefly. To the tester, the elasticity of the four-cylinder motor was especially noteworthy: "Even when you shift into overdrive, there is a very refreshing acceleration, even at 40 kph; in other words, the motor is thoroughly elastic and smooth; yes, one can almost say that silky smoothness is its best overall feature."

The Austin Healey's roadholding was also satisfying, and the interior decor and several other features provided pleasure when driving the lively roadster: "The seats, upholstered in foam rubber (Dunlopille), are very comfortable and suit the body's form very well. The (very high and wide) driveshaft tunnel is also thickly padded. The windshield, which can be folded down very low to the front, is very nice for those who want to go all out, the Rudge spoked wheels with their quick covers are very nice, as are the pleasantly large luggage space and the 55-liter fuel tank."

In 1955 the 100 M (Le Mans) version appeared, made for particularly sporting drivers, with 20 more horsepower. The testers of the English magazine *Motor Sport*, who had already used a 100 as their company car for some time, decided to have it rebuilt into an M version. After two weeks the modifications were finished, and the people of *Motor Sport* were not disappointed when they tried out the car: "The driving characteristics had changed quite astonishingly under all conditions, the car felt considerably more balanced and stable in curves..."

But the improved roadholding was naturally not the only thing that had changed: "With this addition of 20 HP at hand, the overdrive and direct drive are sufficient for normal road driving, and where 100 mph could formerly be attained, now suddenly the speedometer registers 110 mph!" So in the end a thoroughly good grade was given to the Austin Healey: "This car in its present form is a comfortable high-speed car, and as long as the driver does not mistake the road for a race track, it is a safe means of travel too. On long trips in normal traffic conditions, averages of 50 mph can be attained."

In 1956 the Austin Healey gained a six-cylinder motor that produced 100 HP, increased just a year later to 117 HP. Such a car, equipped with overdrive, was taken up by the magazine *The Motor*, to be given a thorough test. At the very beginning there was much enthusiasm for the increased power of the BN6 model: "The additional 17 HP allowed our test car to reach a top speed, measured in both directions, of 108.1 mph... and one could just as easily get down to 15 mph smoothly with this overdrive ratio of 3.18:1, after which the motor was quite willing to accelerate again."

The only negative features were the rather difficult matter of getting in with the top up, the unfortunate seating position for small drivers too close to the steering wheel, and the vulnerability of the exhaust pipe. But several good points were quickly noted, which strengthened the car's positive picture: "Whether one drives the car only normally or definitely sportingly, one always gains from its highly suitable clutch and easy shifting, with overdrive optionally. In city traffic the shift works faultlessly softly, and gives no trouble even in a tough acceleration test from a standing start, and while the shift lever extends through the cockpit in a somewhat unusual way, it proves to work well in the usual manner."

Even the construction of the top, often problematic

Johann Dorfner at the wheel of a Sprite at the Sollböck Mountain Trials in 1959, in which he gained the class victory.

in English roadsters, was judged quite positively: "As already noted, the all-weather equipment of this model proved to be almost 100% effective against water, whether the car was standing still or moving fast, and the side windows also proved to be sufficiently stable."

At the end of the test, the following resume was drawn up:

"Beyond a doubt, the most remarkable thing about this car is its versatility. Without letting one suspect a trace of its temperament, it can rumble through big-city traffic day after day, but when it gets the chance to make the speedometer needle go up quickly, the Austin Healey catapults forward impressively, quite capable of reaching 80 mph after a quarter-mile and 100 after a mile. Finding a comparatively high-performance sports car that is also as comfortable would be possible only among considerably more expensive models."

When in 1959 the Austin Healey 3000 was introduced, with enlarged displacement and 124 horsepower, the same magazine naturally did not miss the chance to test the new type, this time in the 2+2 version with hardtop, and to take the use of the two auxiliary seats into consideration as well: "Though the two back seats looked very small, they are in fact temporarily sufficient for two adults, who are, though, unpleasantly directly exposed to the airstream with the top down. On the other hand, when the hardtop is in place, only small children can fit in."

Naturally there were no complaints about the car,

only the exhaust pipe gave reason for criticism again, since the loud noise was not exactly pleasant, and the volume of noise was increased with the hardtop on.

In mid-1965 the magazine *Automobil* had the chance to drive a rally version of the 3000 Mark III tuned by BMC, which made a remarkable impression on the test driver:

"We want to take a ride in the rally Healey and define the difference. One slithers into the driver's seat and notices how well one is held in place by the seat back. One starts the motor, not touching the gas pedal until it has fired—and gives up all notions of conversation or music from the radio. One steps on the clutch, moves the shift lever to the un-synchronized first gear and drives away softly. (Or one can let in the clutch only at 4000 rpm and fill the air with the smell of burned rubber.) One shifts to second—it may be a little harder if the oil is not warm yet, but then it goes like a hot knife through butter— and the howling noise of the just-meshed gears mixes into the mechanical symphony."

The Mark III marked the endpoint in the development of the big Austin Healey, and when the last of its kind left the factory in 1968, an era of British roadsters came to an end.

In 1958 this powerful sports car was given a sidekick, a Spartan little speedster called the Sprite, better known to us by the nickname "Frogeye". In 1958 a first test appeared in Volume 16 of the magazine *Das Auto, Motor und Sport:*

Again and again in life, one encounters people and things that manage to escape in a mysterious way from a sober judgment of rational estimation. This ability must also be recognized in the little Austin Healey Sprite, and its name of Sprite seems to be not without justification in that respect."

Austin Healey 3000 Mark III, built in 1967.

So the tone was well-meaning at first, but then came the criticism of the frog-eyed car so treasured today: "The form, whose basic styling comes from Pinin Farina, we find pretty and well-done, with one exception that everyone who sees the Sprite criticizes: the headlights. Their position is a makeshift one; they remembered the American regulations that require a minimum height too late, and since they hoped to sell many Sprites in America, there was nothing to do but install them unbeautifully in the engine hood."

The arrangement of the controls was judged as good, but the top came off understandably as bad, as the rain quickly caused an unpleasant dampness in the car. On the other hand, the little motor got good grades on account of its elasticity: "This very sensible design of the motor lets the Sprite be driven particularly speedily and sportily in the speed ranges of normal roads—but less so on the superhighway. There is never a lack of potential for acceleration, the motor is always 'there'." The direct steering and extremely exact shifting also contributed to the tester's feeling of being in a real sports car despite the relatively weak engine power, and saying at the end: "It is an enthusiast's car in the best sense; one does not need to apply the usual strictness in judging it and will gladly overlook its weaknesses."

In 1961 the somewhat more civilized Mark II version appeared, without frog-eyes and with somewhat more power, and *Auto, Motor und Sport* commented in Volume 18, 1961, on the occasion of a test: "The new Mark II remains a Sprite. It has not changed as much from its predecessor as one could conclude from the strongly changed body style; it is only the strange face that irritates." But it irritated in a pleasant way.

The increased power and the more closely spaced gear ratios gave cause for praise; there was disappointment that the chassis had not been reworked, as the car sometimes seemed rather unstable as far as roadholding was concerned. But there were also unpleasant surprises: "The top fit so snugly that even when driving fast in a hard rain, no water came in." All in all, the little roadster had lost none of its fascination, which was expressed in the final comment: "But real roadsters can be compared only with their own kind; the fun of top-down driving cannot be replaced by soft suspension and quiet running, nor the right seat position for driving by soft upholstery, nor handiness by anything. And this fun begins with the Sprite . . ."

In October of 1954 the Motor Show edition of the British magazine *The Autocar* contained this advertisement with the newest record results from Utah.

Austin Healey in Miniature

Austin Healey 100

Schuco Piccolo (D)	Readymade	Diecast	1/90	Cnvrt
Budgie Toys (GB)	Readymade	Diecast	1/76	
Corgi Toys (GB)	Readymade	Diecast	1/43	Cnvrt
Danini/Grand Prix (GB)	Kit	Metal	1/43	Hardtop
Dinky Toys (GB)	Readymade	Diecast	1/43	Cnvrt
Dinky Toys (GB)	Readymade	Diecast	1/43	Competition
K & R Replicas (GB)	Kit	Metal	1/43	
Modsport/Grand Prix (GB)	Kit	Metal	1/43	Hardtop
Schuco Varianto (D)	Readymade	Diecast	1/43*	Cnvrt
Tekno (DK)	Readymade	Diecast	1/43	Cnvrt
Spot-On (GB)	Readymade	Diecast	1/42	Cnvrt
Aurora (USA)	Kit	Plastic	1/32	
Revell (USA)	Kit	Plastic	1/25	
Bandai (J)	Readymade	Tinplate	1/20*	Cnvrt
Bandai (J)	Readymade	Tinplate	1/20*	Hardtop
Tootsietoy (USA)	Readymade	Diecast		

Austin Healey 3000

K & R Replicas (GB)	Kit	Metal	1/43	Mark III
K & R Replicas (GB)	Kit	Metal	1/43	Mark I
Mikansue (GB)	Kit	Metal	1/43	Hardtop
Mikansue Competition (GB)	Kit	Metal	1/43	Rally
Modsport/Grand Prix (GB)	Kit	Metal	1/43	Hardtop
Vitesse (P)	Readymade	Diecast	1/43	Rally
Vitesse (P)	Readymade	Diecast	1/43	Hardtop
Vitesse (P)	Readymade	Diecast	1/43	Top down
Vitesse (P)	Readymade	Diecast	1/43	Top up
Revell (USA)	Kit	Plastic	1/36	
Scalextric (GB)	Readymade	Plas/Met	1/32	
Strombecker (USA)	Kit	Plastic	1/24	

Austin Healey Sprite

K & R Replicas (GB)	Kit	Metal	1/43
Mikansue (GB)	Kit	Metal	1/43
Airfix (GB)	Kit	Plastic	1/32
Monogram (USA)	Kit	Plastic	1/32

Austin Healey Sprite Mark II-IV

Dinky Toys (GB)	Readymade	Diecast	1/43	Cnvrt
K & R Replicas (GB)	Kit	Metal	1/43	Mark II
Mikansue (GB)	Kit	Metal	1/43	

Mikansue Competition (GB)	Kit	Metal	1/43	Sebring 1962
Mikansue Competition (GB)	Kit	Metal	1/43	Mark II Rally
Spot-On (GB)	Readymade	Diecast	1/42	Spider 1962

Austin Healey Le Mans

Bialais (F) 1968	Readymade	Plastic	1/43	Sprite 1300
Grand Prix Models (GB)	Kit	Metal	1/43	Sprite Coupe
RD Marmande (F)	Readymade	Wood	1/43	2 Liter 1955
RD Marmande (F)	Readymade	Wood	1/43	Sprite 1960
RD Marmande (F)	Readymade	Wood	1/43	Sprite 1961
RD Marmande (F)	Readymade	Wood	1/43	Sprite 1964
RD Marmande (F)	Readymade	Wood	1/43	1300 1967

Racing and Record Cars

Morestone (GB)	Readymade	Diecast	1/86	Racing car
Mikansue (GB)	Kit	Metal	1/43	Healey 100 Bonneville 5
Mikansue (GB)	Kit	Metal	1/43	Sprite EX 21 Bonneville 5
Revell (USA)	Kit	Plastic	1/25	Racing car

Healey

Auto Replicas (GB) 1950	Kit	Metal	1/43	Silverstone

Healey Le Mans

RD Marmande (F)	Readymade	Wood	1/43	3.8 L. Coupe
RD Marmande (F) 1952	Readymade	Wood	1/43	4.5 Liter
RD Marmande (F) 1968	Readymade	Wood	1/43	SR 2 Coupe
RD Marmande (F) 1970	Readymade	Wood	1/43	Repco Spider

* approximate scale

International Club Addresses

Austin Healey Club of Sweden
Box 46
S-51404 Tranemo, Sweden

Austin Healey Club of Belgium
Kapitteldreef 70
B-9831 St. Marens Latem, Belgium

Austin Healey Owners Clubs Nederland
Hans Broers
Van Kinsbergenlaan 35
NL Baarn

Midget & Sprite Club
Nigel Williams
7 Kings Avenue
Hanham, Bristol
BS15 3JN, England

Austin Healey Club GB
Mrs. P. C. Marks
171 Coldharbour Road
Bristol BS6 7SX, England

Austin Healey Club Germany
Hirschstrasse 29
D 7500 Karlsruhe, West Germany

British Roadster Club e. V. Düren
Harald Pfeiffer
Am Daens 27
D 5163 Langerwehe-Hamich, West Germany

IG Englischer Sportwagen
K.-H. Schmidt
Neunkirchenweg 85
D 7900 Ulm, West Germany

In almost every country a club is devoted to the care of old Austin Healey sports cars.

Austin Healey Club Schweiz
Ruth Graf
Chilenaustrasse 7
CH 8108 Dällikon, Switzerland

Austin Healey Club Austria
Franz Aigner
Plankenmaisstrasse 20
A 1220 Vienna, Austria

Books for the Austin Healey Fan

The Sprites & Midgets: A Collector's Guide by Eric Dymock. This book covers the smaller Austin Healey models. 112 pages, 140 black and white illustrations, English text.

Austin Healey Cars by R. M. Clarke. The Brooklands Series includes reprints of contemporary road tests and reports, which provide an inclusive picture of the cars of this marque. Each volume 100 pages, very many illustrations, English text: Austin Healey 3000 1959-67, Austin Healey Sprite 1958-71, Austin Healey 100 & 3000—Coll. No. 1 1952-68, Austin Healey Frogeye Sprite—Coll. No. 1 1958-61.

Road & Track on Austin Healey 1953-70. A Brooklands publication with reproductions of contemporary articles. 88 pages, 185 illustrations, English text.

Britische Sportwagen 2 by Halwart Schrader. 2 chapters with 16 pages and 26 b&w and 3 color photos on Austin Healey. In all 168 pages, 351 b/w and 25 color photos. German text.

Automobile Quarterly 17.2 A study of the Austin Healey 100/4 and Le Mans. 10 pages, 7 color photos, some 2-page, English text.

Books for the Austin Healey Fan

Healey by Peter Garnier. The history of Healey and Austin Healey in reprints from the magazine *The Autocar*. Special descriptions, technical studies, road tests, driving impressions, rally and racing results. 160 pages, 350 b/w and 29 color photos, English text.

Austin Healey: The Story of the Big Healeys by Geoffrey Healey. The founder's son has written this inclusive history of this famous English sports-car firm and marque. 256 pages, 200 b/w and 16 color photos, English text.

Healey—The Handsome Brute by Chris Harvey. Along with the developmental history of these models, the technical particulars are also studied. 240 pages, 190 b/w and 20 color photos, English text.

The Big Healeys: A Collector's Guide by Graham Robson. In this popular series there is a volume on the big Healeys, covering the 100/4, 100/6 and 3000. 130 pages, 140 b/w illustrations, English text.

Austin Healey Pocket History. A small but exhaustive and compact guide to the marque. 72 pages, 100 illustrations, some in color, French text.

Die British Motor Corporation ist international und produziert Fahrzeuge verschiedenster Größen und Arten wie kaum eine andere Automobilfabrik. Einen Ausschnitt des PKW-Programmes zeigt die Abbildung, auf der nicht weniger als 41 verschiedene Typen zu sehen sind.
Aber nicht nur Automobile, sondern auch Benzin- und Diesel-motore für die Industrie, Schiffahrt, Landwirtschaft, Bergbau usw. enthält das Programm. Auch Gasturbinen für verschiedenste Zwecke werden hergestellt.
Die BMC verfügt in England über 22 Produktionsstätten:

Longbridge:	Fabrikation von Austin, Morris, Riley PKW's und LKW's
Cowley:	Zusammenbau von Morris und Wolsley-Fahrzeugen — Hauptsitz der Kundendienst Organisation — Nuffield Press Ltd.
Abington:	Zusammenbau von Austin Healey und M.G. Sportwagen
Adderley Park:	Fabrikation von LKW's und Geländewagen
Ward End:	Fabrikation von Achsen und Vorderradaufhängungen
Washwood Heath:	Fabrikation von Karosserien
Erdington:	Fabrikation von SU-Vergasern und Pumpen
Erdington:	Fabrikation von Karosserien und Zubehör
Borderley:	Fahrzeugteile, Plastik
Oxford:	Verchromungswerk, Chrombeschläge, leichte Karosserieteile
Coseley:	Werkausstattg., Fließbänder
Llanelli:	Kinderautos
Bargoed:	Motoren- u. Getriebegehäuse
Wellingborough:	Motoren und Getriebe
Courthouse, Coventry:	Austauschmotoren u. Getriebe
Coventry:	Karosserien
Coventry:	Spezialwerkzeuge
Coventry:	LKW's und Traktoren
Bathgate/Schottland:	Vanden Plas Princess
London:	Luxuswagen
Liverpool:	Waschmaschinen, Fahrräder

Family portrait of British Leyland production in the Sixties, including the Sprite, Midget and Austin Healey 3000.

THE BRITISH MOTOR CORPORATION LTD. BIRMINGHAM UND OXFORD · ENGLAND

Dieses Informationsblatt kann jederzeit ohne Vorankündigung geändert werden. Die gegebenen Informationen sind gültig am Tage der Veröffentlichung dieser Broschüre.

Austin-Alleinimporteur:
A. BRÜGGEMANN & CO GMBH.
DÜSSELDORF, Harffstraße 53
Zweigniederlassung:
HEIDELBERG, Hebelstraße 12

Publ. Nr. BMC 127 D

MG and Austin Healey Spridgets by Chris Harvey. The development from Austin healey Sprite to MG Midget is combined in this very well-equipped book on the marque. 256 pages, 16 in color, more than 200 b/w photos, English text.

Austin Healey "Frogeye" Sprite Super Profile by Lindsay Porter. This volume treats the history, technical development, road tests and club events of the beloved Frogeye Sprite. 56 pages, 90 illustrations, 20 of them in color, English text.

Austin Healey Sprite Mark II/III. Reprint of the original driver's handbook, which also includes data on the Mark II in its appendix. BL A137D. 14 x 21.5 cm, 70 pages, 40 pictures, English text.

Austin Healey Sprite Mark III and Mark IV, Midget Mark II & Mark III Parts Catalogue. Reprint of the spare-parts catalog of February 1977. A4 format, 344 pages, many illustrations, English text.

Austin Healey Sprite Mark IV. Reprint of the original driver's handbook. BL A136D, English text.

Austin Healey Sprite, Midget 1958-1980. Autobooks Repair Guide No. 745, English text.

Austin Healey Sprite Mark I (Frogeye) Owners Handbook. Reprint of the driver's handbook in English, A5 format, 64 pages.

MG Midget/Austin Healey Sprite Roadsters 1958-1974. Haynes Repair Guide No. 265, English text.

Austin Healey 100 Super Profile by John Wheatley. This volume of the Collector Series treats all 4-cylinder models. 56 pages, 90 pictures, 20 in color, English text.

Illustrated Austin Healey Buyers Guide by Richard Newton. In this popular series every model is analyzed and evaluated in detail in terms of its technical particulars and its variations from its predecessor. 152 pages, more than 125 illustrations, English text.

Guide to Purchase and D.I.Y. Restoration of the MG Midget & Austin Healey Sprite by Lindsay Porter. A guidebook for all collectors and owners of these cars who want to restore their vehicles. 200 pages, some 500 illustrations, English text.

Austin Healey 100/4, 100/6, 3000. Spare-parts catalog from Moss Motors Ltd. 14 pages, 70 illustrations.

Austin Healey 100/6 and 3000 (1956-1968). The Complete Official. Reprint of the original factory handbook. A4 format, 408 pages, 367 pictures, English text.

Austin Healey 100/6, 3000 1958-1968. Haynes Repair Guide No. 049, English text.

Austin Healey Sprite Mark II, III und IV sowie MG Midget I, II, III. Reprint of the factory handbook in German. A4 format, WK 626.

Austin Healey Sprite Mark II und III 4-Cyl. Reprint of the factory guidebook. A5 format, WK 1223.